Echoes of a Slient

Goodbye Letter

Dr. Freda Atkins

PRISTINE
PRESS AND MEDIA

ISBN
978-1-964804-34-7 (Paperback)
978-1-964804-35-4 (Hardcover)
978-1-964804-33-0 (eBook)

Dr. Freda Atkins

Echoes of a Silent

TABLE OF CONTENTS

CHAPTER ONE

PRESENT DAY

I can't believe Daniel is dead. Losing a loved one is never easy, but when that loved one is your best friend, it feels like your world is falling apart. That's how I feel right now. My best friend is gone, and I feel like I'm losing my mind.

I can't believe it. I can't accept it. I keep waiting for my friend to come back, to tell me it was all a cruel joke. But that hasn't happened. It is a harsh reality that I must face. My best friend is gone, and my heart is shattered. They say time heals all wounds, but right now, it feels like the wound is just getting deeper and more painful. It is too painful to go back to school and face the very people who loved and then hated him.

They say time heals all wounds, but right now, it feels like the wound is just getting deeper and more painful. It is too painful to go back to school and face the very people who loved and then hated him.

So many thoughts are dancing around in my head when I notice mama chipped ruby red nail polish while she checks her phone as we pull up to a red light. Mama shockingly took the day off work. I am not sure if she is more upset she had to take off work or if she is worried about my mental state. Either way, she has not said more than two words to me as we drive to the counselor's office. My nerves are shot, and my stomach is in knots. I have never been one to openly share my feelings, and the thought of doing so with a stranger is unsettling.

I have always been a very private person, keeping my thoughts and emotions to myself. When I wanted to talk about sensitive things with my parents, like their divorce, it was not welcomed so I keep things to myself. It has always been easier for me to deal with things on my own rather than burdening others with my problems. But now I am starting to have these panic attacks, and I think mama is scared. I am scared.

"I think this is the place," Mama says, pulling up to a stand-alone office. Dr. Emily Dryer, Family and Child Psychologist.

The building stood alone, surrounded by colorful trees and a small garden. The warm red color of the bricks contrasted perfectly with the greenery around it, giving off a welcoming and tranquil vibe. I want to appreciate the rustic and cool feeling of the building but I can't. I think that part of me has been shut off. Disconnected.

"I thought she is counselor like Ms. Khan at school?"

"Psychologists are like counselors, just with more schooling. Now let's go."

I reluctantly get out of the car, walking behind Mama. As I walk closer to the entrance, I notice the intricate details of the building's architecture. The wooden door has a beautiful hand-carved design, and the windows are adorned with delicate lace curtains. This place reminds me of Daniel's house, bougie and fancy.

When I think of a psychologist's office, the image that usually comes to mind is a sterile and clinical setting, filled with bland furniture and neutral colors. However, I am surprised by the color choices of this office. When I walk into the waiting room, I am greeted by the sight of pink velvet chairs and a yellow couch. The softness of the velvet adds a touch of luxury and comfort to the room while the bold pop of yellow adds a fun and playful element.

This combination creates a warm and inviting atmosphere, instantly putting me at ease. The large marble coffee table adorned with an array of magazines ranging from Elle to Hot Wheels, caters to a diverse range of interests. The walls are painted in a soft pink blush, adding a subtle hint of femininity.

"Hello, I'm Ms. Ramsey. My daughter has a ten-thirty appointment."

Mama tells the receptionist who looks young and old at the same time. Trying to distract my thoughts of what is about to happen in this appointment, I try to figure out her age. Maybe she is late thirties or early forties. Her milky skin is smooth, like one of those porcelain dolls Noelle use to collect when we were in elementary school.

Her eyes sparkle with life and vitality, and her smile radiates kindness. Her hair, although slightly greying at the roots, is still thick and full. These are all traits of youth, which adds to the confusion surrounding her age. But as I look closer, I start to notice little details that hint at a different story. Her hands, though small, are adorned with aged spots and prominent veins. There are also faint lines around her eyes and mouth, indicating a life of laughter and joy or maybe one of worry and stress. Oh God will I look young and old too because of my stress?

Between the office design and the receptionist, my mind is wondering what I got myself into. Who is this lady? But I do not have to wait long to find out. When a woman with a red mullet comes out and greets us, Mama's mouth hit the ground first as we both are taken aback by the sight of this woman. I stare at her unique sense of style. She is wearing a pair of skinny, black jeans and a striped V-neck shirt, paired with an oversized blazer, all of which seem to exude confidence and individuality. Her whole demeanor screams big city, nothing like Coral Bluff.

As I look her up and down, my eyes are drawn to her feet, where a pair of black Doc Martens complete her look. It is then that I realize the true extent of her fashion sense. This woman is not just following the latest trends, she is creating her own style and owning it with pride.

"Hello, you must be Andrea." Dr. Dyrer's smile, along with her fire engine red hair, lights up the room. "And you must be Ms. Ramsey. I'm Dr. Dryer, but you can call me Dr. E."

"I go by Drea."

"Cool beans, Drea. Are you ready to get started?"

"Um, don't I sit in on the session?" Mama asks, clearing her throat. She is as surprised at this whole interaction as I am. "I mean, she is a minor."

"I prefer to see my clients without their parents because they seem to open up more to a non-biased person, but I will give that choice to you, Drea. Would you like your mother to sit in your session?"

I look at Mama and back at Dr. E. I do not feel threatened or uneasy.

"I'm good, Mama. You don't have to sit in with me."

A little disappointment flashes across mama's eyes, but she stays strong. "Okay, I'll be out here waiting on you."

"Cool beans. Let's go back to my office, Drea."

Her bubbly personality is almost annoying, but it feels oddly genuine. Which is so weird because I do not think I have ever met anyone who is this damn happy.

Her office is an extension of the whimsical color choices she has around the lobby. She has a blush pink accent wall behind her desk. The furniture, including a desk and bookshelf, is white with gold accents, adding a touch of sophistication.

"Please have a seat, Drea. Would you like something to drink? Water or juice?"

Dr. E asks pointing towards a mini fridge on the side of her organized desk.

"No, thank you."

Dr. E pulls out a hot pink notebook with a candy cane pen, making me giggle to myself, which is strange because I cannot remember the last time I laughed.

"Is, everything okay Drea?"

"Yes, ma'am."

"Oh, you don't have to call me ma'am. My mother is a ma'am. I'm just Dr. E."

"Ummm okay."

"So tell me a little bit about yourself and why you came to see me."

I move around in my chair before sitting on my hands. I do not know this lady from a can of paint, and although she dresses well and has a cool office, I still do not know her.

"I'm a sophomore at Oak Valley High School. And I'm pretty smart."

"Okay, and what else?" "I don't know."

"You don't know what?"

"I don't know what you want me to say."

"Say whatever is on your mind." "I can't."

"Why not?"

"Because adults always say tell me how I feel and what's on my mind, And when I do share my feelings, they get mad at me. So, I'd rather not say anything."

"Well, I don't know about the other adults to whom you're referring, but I know myself, and I just want to hear your truth."

"Why?"

"Because I may be able to help you sort through whatever you may be going through."

"I doubt it."

"Try me."

"Ugh, this is so stupid. I really don't want to be here." "Why not?"

"Because I can figure this stuff out on my own."

"Are you sure? Because your body language toward your mom seemed distant, which tells me you don't feel heard at home. And your body language right now suggests that you are open to this meeting, and you don't feel threatened by me. Plus, didn't you have a panic attack at school. Isn't that the reason why you're here?" She pauses for a minute. "But you still don't know if you can trust me.

And I'm not sure if it's because you think I'm this rocker white chick or I'm a total stranger asking to get in your business." Her subtle smile disarms me.

"I guess a little bit of both. How did you do that?"

"Do what?"

"Figure all that out through body language."

"I study people for a living. That's how I can help them."

I readjust myself in the chair, placing my hands in my lap. I take in a deep breath and exhale slowly. "I lost one of my best friends to suicide." I look down at my Air Force Ones because I can not face her.

Tears rush to my eyes and fall, hitting the top of my shoes. Dr. E hands me several tissues. When I finally look up, her face has no emotion. Not happiness. Not sadness. Not even judgment.

"Would you like to take a break, Drea?"

"No, I'm good. I cry every time I talk or think about Daniel, which is pretty much every day."

"Why are you angry?"

"I didn't say I was angry."

"Your body tensed up when you mentioned Daniel's suicide."

"Oh, I didn't realize it. I don't know. I guess because we talked the day before and I thought he was in a good space. I found out the next day he took his life. He left me. He didn't even say goodbye or anything."

"I know this must have been difficult for you to share, but I want to say thank you for trusting me enough to share your feelings with me." She pauses for a minute and taps her candy cane pen against her notebook. "Drea, anger is not an easy emotion to understand. It's complex and often holds deeper roots than what we are aware of. Sometimes parents or society teach us to suppress our feelings, especially anger. We are told it isn't ladylike to be angry and that we should always maintain a calm demeanor. But anger is much more than a physical reaction. It also holds valuable information about our emotional state. Think of it like a warning sign that alerts us to potential problems that need to be addressed. For example, if we feel angry because we were not given credit for our work, it may be a sign that we value recognition and fairness. If we get angry when someone interrupts us, it may be a sign that we value respect and attentiveness. Do you understand?"

"You mean the anger I feel is normal and it's telling me something else about myself?"

"Yes," Dr. E says, leaning forward in her chair. "By paying attention to our anger and understanding its underlying causes, we can learn more about ourselves and our needs. It can also help us communicate with others in a more effective way. Often, our anger is a result of unmet expectations or unexpressed feelings. By acknowledging and addressing these underlying issues, we can work toward finding a resolution instead of reacting in anger."

"Well, what is my underlying issue?"

"You tell me. You said you and Daniel spoke the day before he committed suicide. You thought everything was fine, but it wasn't."

"Oh my God. Am I mad at Daniel?"

"Are you?"

"I think I am." I bury my face into my hands. "I can't believe it. All this time. But why?"

"Could it be Daniel made a choice based on how the situation affected him? Or maybe because he didn't tell you his plan before he did it. Either way, you may have felt excluded from his plan and perhaps his life."

I sit in shock. Her words are mind boggling but make so much sense. And for the first time, my emotions are starting to make sense.

"Our time is just about up, but I'll see you again Wednesday.

That is if you want to come back." "Yes, of course."

"Oh, Drea? Tonight, I want you to write a letter."

"A letter? About what and to who?" "To Daniel."

"Daniel? But he is dead."

"I want you to write a letter expressing your forgiveness to him. How you felt shut out from his life when he made the decision to end his. Be honest and transparent. You don't have to share it with anyone if you don't want to. This is more for you."

Taking a deep exhale, I think the assignment is strange, but this is the best I've felt since Daniel's death. "Okay, Dr. E. I'll do it."

CHAPTER TWO

AUGUST 2022

The first day of school had always been a big deal for my best friends, Harmony and Noelle. Ever since fifth grade, we've had this tradition of walking to school together. It's a small thing, but it meant the world to me. We always met at my house because I lived closer to the school. As we walked, we talked about our summer and made predictions about the new school year. One of the highlights of our first day ritual was taking a picture together before we left my house. It had become a tradition to capture our excitement and nervousness before walking into a new school year. We made silly faces and pose with our backpacks. Looking back at these pictures at the end of the school year was always a laugh. It was amazing to see how much we'd changed in just one year.

Buzz.

As I reached for my phone and pulled it out from under the covers, I already knew who it was before I answer.

"Hey!"

"Hey, girl! You ready? Noelle is already headed to school."

"I thought we were going to walk together like we always do on the first day of school," I said, already feeling a slight disappointment. Too much was changing, and I didn't like it. We missed the first day of school meetup last year too because Harmony was homeschooled.

"Are you meeting me at my house?" I was hoping Harmony would say yes because I wasn't ready to let go of our traditions.

"Yeah. I'll meet you at your house."

"Will we have time to take our first day pictures?"

"I don't think so. I have to say my goodbyes to Matthew.
Besides, Noelle won't be in it."

"Whatever. I'll see you when you get here. I have to finish getting dressed."

"Aww. Don't be mad. I'll see you in a few."

I laced up my favorite sneakers and made sure I had all of my school supplies in my backpack. I couldn't help but feel a sense of excitement and anticipation for the upcoming school year. After surviving the turmoil of my freshman year, I was determined to make my sophomore year the complete opposite. I wanted it to be a year filled with growth, success, and memorable experiences. Just because the trio wasn't walking into Oak Valley High School together, it didn't mean it was going to be a bad year.

I did a quick look-over. I made sure my baby hairs were neatly laid, framing my smooth mahogany brown face perfectly to accentuate my new Fulani braids. Feeling confident and ready to take on the day, I picked up my backpack and waited for Harmony.

Heading out to meet Harmony on the porch, I saw the finely written note my mom loved to leave around the house. She recently started leaving more and more notes with funny sayings or reminders or my list of chores since she had increased her hours at the hospital.

Drea, I know this school year is going to be your best year yet. I'm sorry I couldn't be home to see you and your friends off. I'm working a double shift today so I'll be home in the morning. You have the leftovers in the fridge. -Love, Mom.

I left the note on the kitchen table and saw Harmony walking up my porch. I set the house alarm and locked the door.

"Are those new Jordans, Harmony?"

Harmony was known for her sneaker collection, which she took very seriously.

"Well, kinda. I had to get another pair of Jordan 1s because my last pair had too many scuff marks and crease at the top. But I see you got them new Travis Scott's. Since when you started wearing good sneakers?"

"Oh, really? Seriously?"

"Seriously! You never cared about name-brand sneakers."

"I don't know. Franklin told Mama he wanted some new sneakers for his birthday, and she bought me a pair too."

"So you should be thanking your brother for putting you on game."

"Oh, shut up. Anyway, why didn't Ms. Noelle want to walk with us? Is the princess too good to walk with the peasants now?" I said with my best rendition of a British aristocrat voice.

Laughing at my horrible accent, Harmony said, "No, but one would think that. She had some type of orientation meeting for the cheer squad at 7:30 this morning."

"Dang. Why so early?"

"Hell if I know. I just know as the co-captain she had to be there."

Noelle has been cheering since she was three years old. Her parents idolized her. Well, her mother for sure idolized her along with everybody at Oak Valley. It's not every day you saw a fair skin Black girl with green eyes in Coral Bluff, Alabama. Her look was exotic, and she knew it, which made her attitude more spicy.

"Are you nervous about the new year?" I asked without trying to seem obvious.

"No, not really. I mean, not that much has changed."

"Yeah, but are you glad to be coming back to school and not be homeschooled anymore?"

"I guess, but this is going to be the first time I'm going to be away from Matthew for more than six hours. I miss my baby."

I watched my feet move in front of the other because I didn't know what to say. Last year was a hard transition for me and not just because I was starting high school. I started high school without Harmony. But she must have sense my reluctance to ask more about Matthew because she changed the subject.

"Are you nervous about starting all advanced honors classes? You won't have the same class schedule with Noelle anymore. Do we even have the same lunch period?"

"I think so. I have lunch during sixth period, after advanced geometry.

"I have lunch during fifth period, but I'll hang around before the late bell ring to catch up with you."

"And we're still walking home together? Hopefully with Noelle?"

After chuckling, Harmony says, "If she's not too busy for us."

By the time we reached the school, there were so many students hanging outside, trying not to let their nerves get the best of them. There was so much pressure one felt as a high schooler. It was just not about having on the freshest pair of sneakers anymore. You had to make sure your hairstyles matched your outfits too. And when posting, you had to make sure you used the right filter and music in your posts. And you had to be able to capture the moments friendship, more like sistership. Sometimes it felt like a never- ending cycle I wished I could get out of.

"I'll catch you after school."

"Okay. Wish me luck with my new classes."

"Girl, you don't need any luck. You're like the smartest student in this freaking school."

"Aww, thanks Harmony. You always know how to gas me up."

"It's the truth. But I'll see you later."

Walking through the hallways toward my locker made me think about the previous year. It was a rollercoaster of emotions— from Harmony going out with the worst boy Alabama had ever produced and getting pregnant by him to my own family breaking up right before my eyes. There were times when I felt lost and unsure of myself, and I still felt that way at times. And now, I was proud of my growth and resilience. This new school year represented a fresh start for me. I had set goals for myself and was determined to achieve them. This year, I was maintaining a high GPA and might get involved in extracurricular activities. I was ready to put in the hard work so I can get into the University of Chicago or Northwestern.

"Welcome back, Drea,"Oliver said from behind my locker.

He was about a foot shorter than me so he couldn't look over the top of the locker.

"Thanks, Oliver."

"I didn't see much of you this summer."

"Yeah, I was busy." "Busy doing what?"

Oh my goodness. Why was he asking me a thousand and one questions? Rolling my eyes, I said, "Spending time in Chicago and preparing for the new year."

"I hope we are in the same classes this year again."

The plastered grin on his face was all too familiar. He had that same dorky smile since second grade when he professed his love to me during our class Valentine's party. The only difference now was the metal from his braces were covering his crooked chiclet teeth.

"We probably won't." "Why not?"

His obnoxious grin of optimism faded.

"I'm taking all advanced honors classes this year." "Look at my girl."

"Oliver, I'm not your girl."

Ignoring my comment, he proceeded, "You've always been smart. When is your lunch period? Or I can walk you home after school."

"I have lunch during sixth period, and I always walk home with Harmony and Noelle, you know that."

"Well, there was no Harmony last year. Is she back?" The bell rang.

"Gotta go. Can't be late for class." I was already halfway down the hall.

When I walked into my new homeroom class, I was greeted by familiar faces. Some from last year and some I've never thought would test into advanced honors like Ms. Paisley Moreno. I assumed she was more interested in competing with Noelle on who can get the most popular guys to ask them out.

"Alright, everyone. Take your seat," Mrs. Holmer said, looking over what's sure to be designer red glasses. Mrs. Holmer always dressed so nicely, matching her glasses with every outfit. She was young, energetic, and just the right amount of flavor to let you know her four-foot-eleven stature was nothing to mess with.

"This will be your homeroom for the remainder of your high school career or as long as you're in advanced honor classes."

Sitting mid-row, of course behind ass-kisser Paisley, I was reminded what was at stake this school year. I knew that it wouldn"t be a smooth-sailing journey. There would be challenges and obstacles along the way. But I was ready to face them head on. I was determined to maintain my grades so I could get a scholarship and leave this slow town.

Mrs. Holmer continued, "After I do roll call, we will go over the expectations of staying in the advanced honors classes and what it means for your future endeavors."

"Excuse me, Mrs. Holmer," Principal Thomas said, standing in the doorway. "You have one more student who has been added to the advanced honors class."

"So I now have twenty-three students?" she asked, shifting her weight from one side to the other in her four-inch heels.

"Yes, he was a late transfer student, but I have just received his test results and last year's grades so he's good to go." Sighing while pushing up her glasses, she said, "Okay, honey, please come in and take your seat. What's your name?"

"Daniel Gardner, ma'am."

"Nice to meet you, Daniel. You can take the seat next to Andrea."

Mrs. Holmer said pointing to the empty seat next to me.

Love at first sight is often considered a myth, a concept that exists only in fairy tales and romantic comedies. However, as I sat frozen in my seat, my heart skipped a beat, and I knew then that love at first sight was indeed real. It was the moment when Daniel walked through the door and into my life, bringing with him a feeling of excitement and anticipation that I had never felt before. I had always been skeptical about love at first sight, especially when Harmony thought she was in love last year and all he did was cheat and mistreat her.

I believed that love was something that developed over time as two people got to know each other and formed a deep connection. But who's to say that it would last? My parents did not last. But as soon as I saw Daniel, all my doubts vanished. The cliché of time standing still suddenly became a reality for me. My thoughts stopped, my heart raced, and I simply couldn't take my eyes off him. Daniel was the epitome of perfection, his glowing sandalwood complexion radiating. He had a tall, toned body and full lips. This man was gorgeous. Every movement he made walking to his seat exuded confidence and charm. As he walked toward me, with a smile playing on his lips, I couldn't help but feel drawn by his presence. It's funny how one single moment can change your entire life. In that brief encounter, my heart made the decision for me; Daniel was the one.

It felt like I had known him all my life, like our souls were connected in some strange way. I knew then and there that I wanted to get to know this perfect boy who had just entered my life.

"Hello, I'm Daniel," he said, taking the seat next to me. "Hi."

Hi? That's all I can say? Am I stupid or something? That's the best thing I can say?

"Mrs. Holmer." "Yes, Paisley?"

"I like to elect myself to be the advanced honors class ambassador and show Daniel around until he's comfortable."

Are you serious? Perfect Paisley swooped in and elected herself to show Daniel around like she owned the school, acting like she was better than everyone else. Why? Just because she was beautiful with her big loose curls and caramel skin tone, which highlights her Puerto Rican and Black heritage. And she was always quick to remind us of her ethnicity, as if that defined her worth as a person. But let's be real here, being mixed does not automatically make you better than anyone else. In fact, it's not even something that you have control over. It is a part of who you are, not something that gives you a free pass to act like a diva.

"Sure, that sounds like a good idea. You two can get together after class."

Really? Was the universe conspiring against me? Just when I was working up the nerve to introduce myself, here came Paisley.

One more thing I had to deal with.

CHAPTER THREE

The first day of school went by so fast it was almost a blur except for you, Daniel. I couldn't wait to see you again and get to know you more. Our first encounter was brief, yet it left a lasting impression on me. I found myself wanting to know more about your thoughts, your dreams, and everything that makes you who you were. But most of all, I couldn't wait to see the real side of you that I knew was captivating.

Every step I took toward the front entrance, I felt a smile inching onto my face from the thought of Daniel until it was rudely interrupted.

"I miss not seeing you in my classes," Oliver said, walking behind me in the hallway with his book bag swallowing him. "My day seemed to move slower when you're not around."

"Sorry, Oliver." I spotted Harmony and Noelle near the school's entrance. "I gotta go. I'll catch up with you later."

"If you give me your number, I can call you later." Pretending to not hear his last request, I threw my hand up without looking back.

"Whew, you guys saved me." I slowed down, trying to catch my breath.

Adjusting her crossbody purse, Noelle said, "Why were you running?"

"Oliver Greene."

"I have English Lit with him," Harmony said. "He asked me about you."

"Ugh! He's so annoying."

"Aww, Drea. I think it's cute. He's liked you since forever."

"So? It doesn't mean I have to like him back," I said, rolling my eyes.

"All I'm saying is he's nice guy who really likes you."

"And what makes you the expert on men, Harmony?" Noelle liked to make sly comments or questions when she wanted to be messy, even with her friends. "Have you ever been in love?"

Harmony stopped walking, turned, and looks at Noelle. "Excuse me?"

"I mean, you haven't had much experience with guys." "You mean I haven't slept with as many boys as you?"

"I ain't no ho."

"Ladies, ladies, ladies." I interjected myself in between the two of them. "Why are we arguing with each other? We haven't seen that much of each other over the summer, and we don't have classes with each other this year. Can we just get along?"

"She started it," Harmony said as she started walking backward.

"She's right, Noelle. You came for Harmony for no reason."

"My bad. Damn. Y'all so sensitive."

Harmony sucked her teeth and rolled her eyes because we were both familiar with Noelle's half-ass apologies.

"Anyway, have either of y'all seen the new guy, Daniel?" I said with more excitement in my voice than I realized.

"Yeah, I heard there was some cute guy who transferred." Noelle said. "Why? You've seen him?"

"He's in all of my classes." I smiled. I felt a wave of happiness and embarrassment wash over me at the same time. "Somebody's extra excited." Harmony lightly elbowed me. "No, I'm not. I was just letting you two know that he's in all of my classes."

"Uh-huh." Harmony searched my eyes to see if I was telling the truth. "Well, I haven't heard a thing about him."

"I heard Paisley has already sunk her teeth into him."

"Wait, what?" I stopped and pulled on Noelle's arm.

"What do you mean Paisley already has her teeth in him? Did you see them kiss?"

Noelle and Harmony looked at each other and burst into laughter. And just like that, they were over their tiff, at my expense, of course. My lack of knowledge and experience with boys was a joke to them.

"Stop laughing at me." I could feel the embarrassment return.

"It's just a figure of speech, silly. Girl, you really need to get your head out of those books and talk to a boy for once," Noelle said, laughing while trying to form her sentences.

"Paisley sees something she wants, and she gets it. No one really tells her no."

Harmony must have noticed I wasn't smiling or was even amused at the news. "Drea, you good?" "Yeah. I mean, I guess so."

"What's wrong?"

"Yeah, What's up with you?" Noelle said behind Harmony.

"I don't know. I mean, nothing. I just thought Daniel was cute. It's not a big deal."

But it was a big deal for me. Deep down, I knew Daniel wouldn't look twice at me. Paisley was everything I wasn't: confident, outgoing, and beautiful in a way that could turn heads. I couldn't help but feel threatened by her presence, especially when I saw how easily she could captivate everyone's attention, including Daniel's.

"Well, since it's no big deal, you shouldn't mind if Paisley talked to him or not," Harmony said, stopping at the corner where she and Noelle could cut through and get to their house. "I gotta get home to relieve Granny and play with Matthew. We'll see you tomorrow, Drea."

"Later," I said, walking across the street to my home.

The fiery hot sun pierced my scalp, causing beads of sweat to trickle down from my Fulani braids. Walking home, I couldn't shake what Noelle said about Paisley. If Noelle already knew about Paisley and Daniel, then it was sure a done deal for me. Plus, I didn't get to ask them my questions.

Making my way up my porch and into my house, I dropped my bookbag down and let out a sigh. Home was meant to be a place of warmth and comfort, a sanctuary from the chaos of the outside world. It was a place where we could truly be ourselves, surrounded by the things and people we love. It was where memories were made, and where we found comfort in times of turmoil. However, my home no longer held that meaning for me. I walked into my house, and I was greeted by an eerie silence quite different from the lively atmosphere that once filled it. The walls that were once decorated with family photos now stood bare, reminding me of the void left behind by Daddy and Franklin.

The familiar sound of music and laughter had been replaced by the constant beep of the microwave and the distant hum of the refrigerator. The absence of my family was hard to accept, as each room reminded me of the cherished moments we shared. The living room, where we would gather for movie nights, now felt hollow and uninviting. The kitchen, where delicious aromas once danced in my nose hairs from my mama and daddy's cooking, now felt like a stranger's domain. And my bedroom, which used to be my sanctuary, now only brought a sense of loneliness and longing. The emptiness left behind by my family's absence seemed to have seeped into every corner of my home.

I warmed up the leftover meatloaf, mashed potatoes, and sweet peas in the microwave. By the time the microwave beeped, signaling completion, Mama called.

"Hey, Ma." I put her on speaker so I could have free hands to get my meal out.

"Hey, honey bunny. How was your first day of school?"

"It was good."

"How are your advanced honor classes? Do you think you'll be able to handle it?"

"Yes, I can handle it." I really hated my mama's questions.

They felt disingenuous. "When are you coming home?" "Did you get my note? I'm working a double today." "Yeah, I saw your note."

"Baby, you know I'm only doing this for a short period." Yeah, she said that last year when she went back to work.

She's at work more than she is at home with me.

"Yes, ma'am, I know."

"I have to go; they are calling me. Don't forget to brush your teeth before bed."

She hung up before I could agree to her request.

CHAPTER FOUR

Paisley and Daniel. A match made in heaven, or so it seemed. Over the next few days, they had been inseparable, joined at the hip like two peas in a pod. The constant note passing and laughing at inside jokes in class was hard to ignore and enough to make my stomach hurt. Everywhere I went, there they were - whispering sweet nothings, making goo-goo eyes, and constantly giggling. It was enough to make anyone want to gag. Although I wish it was me. I really wanted it to be me.

Paisley's constant public displays of affection went beyond the realm of normalcy. I'd never seen her like this before, even when she dated Marcus Hoover, co-captain of our varsity basketball team. It was almost as if she were trying to prove something to the world, to show off her ability to get whatever she wanted.

My eyes automatically rolled whenever I was around her. I add a little sucking of my teeth when Paisley and Daniel were both around. This was a hard act to keep up since we had every class together. And today didn't make any difference. Walking into Mr. Fitzgerald's science class, the terrifying thought of seeing those two for the next three years of my high school career was torture.

"Settle down class. Settle down," Mr. Fitzgerald said. looking like an extra in the show High School Musical.His fair creamy skin color was washed out against his. Hues of lavender and soft blues seemed to be his favorite color choices. Dark-frame glasses highlighted his electric blue eyes. "Everyone, take your seats."

We all took our seats, and, of course, the two love birds sat next to each other.

"As we discussed on the first day of school, everyone will be graded based upon their semester's project, your own electric ropeway, an endless aerial cable moved by a stationary engine and used to transport freight such as logs. You will be paired with one of your classmates."

Small chatter erupted as everyone was anxious on who they would choose for their partner. And since we were all technically smart, the decision lay in popularity.

"Quiet down. I have already paired you all up."

I couldn't help but feel a little nervous about who my partner for the class would be. Science was never my strongest suit, and having a good partner was crucial for my success in this class. The anticipation of whom I would be paired with for the next few months was almost unbearable. I would rather eat a live spider than be paired with Paisley.

"When I call your pair name, please go and sit by them.

Maranda and Jeannie. Virginia and Leo. Chris and Jennifer. Andrea and Daniel."

Mr. Fitzgerald continued to speak over the disgruntle sighs from the students. Did I hear him correctly? I was going to be partnered with Daniel? Fate had a funny way of working things out.

I couldn't indulge in my thoughts for long. Daniel was walking toward the empty seat next to me. Oh my God, I could feel my heart racing, and my hands quickly sweated. What do I say? Oh God, I hope my breath does not stink. I knew I should not have eaten that cream cheese bagel.

"Looks like we're going to be science partners," Daniel said, flashing a grin in my direction.

I smiled back, feeling a flutter in my stomach. As soon as Mr. Fitzgerald announced our new semester partners, I wanted to text the girls, but I couldn't.

Daniel walked over to my lab table and plopped his books on his stool.

"I hope you're good in science," Daniel said, looking back at Paisley, whose eyes were laser-focused on us.

"I'm okay, but I always pull my weight."

"That's good to know. Do you go by Andrea or Drea?"

Oh my goodness! He knows my name? I didn't even think he noticed anyone outside of Paisley.

"Drea is fine." The way I kept my cool was a miracle because my insides were doing somersaults.

"Alright, class. Settle down. I will cover the project requirements and my expectations. You all can meet and work on your projects during class, but the best use of your time would be after school. " Mr. Fitzgerald said, placing one packet on each of our tables.

"We can meet after school. I live about fifteen minutes away from here in the Meadow Hills neighborhood."

"I live only a few minutes away." I pointed toward the window in the direction of my home. "I'm right down the street."

"Oh, that's perfect. I can just come to your house, and we can work on the project together."

Did he just invite himself over to my house? How did I go from watching Paisley take the love of my life to the love of my life coming over to my house to hang out? Well, more like work on our school project. But who cared about that? The fact that Daniel would be in my realm was mind-blowing.

"That works. I'll let my mom know." "Perfect! We can start this afternoon." "Today?"

"Yeah. Why not? We only have nine weeks to complete this project."

For one, my house was a mess. I hadn't cleaned up in a few days, and it was starting to show. I knew I should've done something about it, but I just couldn't seem to find the motivation. By the time I came home, all I wanted to do was collapse on the couch and binge- watch my favorite shows. Secondly, I was not the most organized person. In fact, I was pretty sure the word "messy" was created with someone like me in mind. I tried to cleanup as I went, but it never seemed to be enough. Saturdays used to be our designated cleaning day. We would each pick two rooms in the house and see who would clean their area the fastest. Daddy would always win. And now it was just me and Mama, the daily house chores seemed to escaped us both.

"Yeah, you have a point. Sure. I'll meet you in the front after school. We can walk to my house."

"I'll meet you there."

Nervousness settled in my stomach, giving me a queasy feeling.

After last period, I skipped the usual locker run and head straight to the front of the school. Standing outside, fidgeting with my charm bracelet, I couldn't help but feel a sense of dread wash over me. My mind was consumed with thoughts of Daniel, and I felt my stomach turning again as I anxiously waited for him. But now, with every passing minute that Daniel was not here, my nerves seemed to be getting the best of me. I can't stop replaying all the different scenarios in my head. What if he didn't show up? What if the conversation was awkward? I took a deep breath, trying to calm my racing heart. But it was no use; the anticipation was almost suffocating.

"I'm surprised you beat Harmony and me out," Noelle said, walking up to me and pulling her hair up in bun. The curls on the nape of her neck was sweated and glued down. "Ugh, it doesn't matter what texture your hair is, the humidity here is brutal."

"I'm meeting Daniel so we can work on our science project." I couldn't believe those words were coming out of my mouth. They just came out like vomit.

"Daniel?" Noelle rubbed the excess product from her hair onto the side of her pants.

Before I could explain, Harmony walked up. "Y'all ready?" "I'm ready, but Ms. Drea over here isn't. She's waiting for D- a-n-i-e-l to come out so they can work on their 'science project.'" Noelle said, enunciating every letter in Daniel's name.

"Oh really?" Harmony sinister smile didn't put me at ease.

"Now I need to know all the tea."

"Hello, ladies." As if this situation couldn't get more uncomfortable, Oliver walked out before Daniel. "Hey, Drea."

"Hey, Oliver." I checked my phone for the time, hoping Daniel would come out sooner rather than later. I felt a mixture of excitement and fear building up inside of me.

"Do you have any plans this weekend? There's a new Marvel movie coming out." Oliver ignored Noelle and Harmony and focused on my response to his millionth offer to take me out.

"Yeah, Drea? What are your plans this weekend or this evening?" Harmony jokingly asked while Noelle laughed.

Oliver looked at the girls and back at me. "So do you have plans?"

I saw Daniel walking toward me with a big smile on his face.

My heart beat faster, and my mouth became annoyingly dry. My thoughts raced. How could I end this conversation quickly?

"Hey. I'm Daniel," he said, walking up to me. Daniel's presence radiated warmth and positivity to everyone. His impeccable fashion sense was just one aspect of Daniel's personality that drew Noelle's admiration, Harmony's approval, and Oliver's hatred.

"I'm Oliver," he said with a tone of voice that conveyed assertiveness without coming across overly-aggressive.

I rolled my eyes. Oliver was so extra.

"I'm Harmony, and this is Noelle," Harmony said, nudging Noelle.

"These are my two best friends," I said, pointing to Harmony and Noelle.

"And who am I?" Oliver asked, trying to insert himself into the conversation yet again.

"Oliver is a friend. Now can we go?"

"I'm following you," Daniel said, stepping back so I could lead the way.

"I guess I'll catch you later, Drea." There was a hint of disappointment in Oliver's voice.

"See you," I said with sweet relief. That situation could have gone much worse. But luckily my words came out faster than my thoughts and no one was offended Everything happened so fast, and now Daniel was walking home with the girls and me.

Walking home with my two besties and my crush was something I could never have dreamed of. It was like a scene straight out of a movie, and I couldn't believe that it was actually happening to me.

As we casually walked down the familiar street leading to my home, I couldn't help but be worried and concerned. Will we only talk about the science project? Will he judge my messy house? Did I put on enough deodorant?

"How do you like living in Coral Bluff?" Harmony asked to break the awkward silence.

"It's cool."

"Where're you from?" I'm so glad Harmony asked the questions. I didn't ask because I was wondering if I had gum in my bookbag.

"I'm from Elkhorn, Tennessee, a small town about two hundred miles west of Nashville."

"Looks like I need to visit Elkhorn." Noelle flashed a flirtatious smile on her fair face.

Ignoring the flirtatious tone of Noelle's comment, Daniel rubbed the back of his neck. "Yeah, there's not much there."

"Well, this is the street we take to get to our house," Harmony said, stopping at the corner. "I'll text you later, Drea."

"Yeah, me too," Noelle chimed in.

"See y'all later," I said with the reality of me and Daniel being alone settling in.

The warm evening air brushed against my skin, and the sun painted the sky in shades of orange and pink. It was the perfect end to a perfect day.

"This is it," I said, taking out my keys. I saw Mama's car in the driveway so she's either sleeping or on the phone talking to Aunt Jolie, her younger sister.

But she was doing neither. When we walked into my house, I noticed mama sitting on the sofa, looking like a zombie. Her tired expression, droopy eyes, and slumped posture told me that working back-to-back double shifts at the hospital was catching up to her. I knew how hard she had been working ever since the pandemic hit, but the pandemic was over. As a neonatal nurse, she was at the forefront of the battle against COVID-19, and her dedication and hard work were truly commendable. But it also meant that she was constantly putting her own health and well-being at risk, working long hours and dealing with the increasing number of patients every day. Plus, she was never home anymore. I knew Mama was important as a nurse, but I needed her too as my mama.

I walked toward her and sat down next to her on the sofa. "Hey, Mom. How was work today?" I asked, already knowing the answer.

She let out a tired sigh and leaned her head back against the cushion. "Exhausting," she replied in a hoarse voice. "And who is your friend?"

"Hello, ma'am. I'm Daniel." He reached out his hand to shake Mama's hand, but she closed her eyes while he was talking.

He politely puts his hand back into his pockets.

"You need me to do anything?" I asked, knowing she was going to say no. That was my mama, the real independent Joan of Arc type of lady.

"No. No. I just want to sit and relax. You can order a pizza for you and your friend." Getting up from the sofa, she saiad, "I'm going to take me a long hot bath and get in bed. It was nice meeting you, Daniel."

"Nice meeting you too, ma'am."

Feeling a little embarrassed, I knew Mama was going to be tired, but she almost came off rude. I bet Paisley's parents were nicer to him. Had he met her parents?

I must have had an uneasy look on my face, but it didn't seem to bother Daniel. He turned to me and said, "So what kind of pizza are we ordering before we hit the books?"

And just like that, our friendship was formed.

CHAPTER FIVE

PRESENT DAY

There are times when putting pen to paper is the hardest thing to do. For me, it is even harder when it comes to writing about my feelings. But today, I am faced with a challenge: writing a forgiveness letter to Daniel. Believe me when I say the struggle is real. How do I begin to write a letter forgiving someone who is not here to defend himself or even hear it? How do I put into words the anger and frustration I feel toward him? These questions have been swirling in my mind since leaving Dr. E's office, and I still have not come up with a satisfying answer. I never thought I would be in this position. Daniel was someone I trusted and loved deeply. We had a strong relationship built on mutual understanding and respect. But then, he did the one thing I never thought he would do: he broke my trust and shattered my heart. I could accept the fact he turned from my crush to best friend. But I could not accept the fact he took his life.

"Drea, are you ready to go?"

"One minute. I'll be right out."

Placing my pen down on an empty page, I put on my gym shoes and met Mama at the front door. "You ready, honey?"

"Yes, ma'am, I am."

"Wait a minute." Mama stepped back to observe my face. "What is it? Do I have something on my face?"

"Yeah, you do."

"What is it?" I go to the mirror over our sofa to inspect my face, but I do not see any pimples, eye boogers, or ashy lips. "I don't see anything."

"I do. I see a glimmer of hope in your eyes. The first time in a long time."

"Ugh, Mama. Seriously? You scared me for a minute."

"I was scared too but longer than a minute. Come on. Let's go."

I settle into the front seat of our car, and I feel a sense of anticipation bubbling up inside of me. It is a strange feeling, considering the last time I was on this same route, I was a bundle of nerves and anxiety. But now, as we drive toward Dr. E's office, the knots that once were in my stomach were replaced with butterflies of excitement. In one session, I was able to sleep throughout the night without waking up in tears or sweat. To me, that was progress because of the help of Dr. E.

We pull up to the familiar building, and I take a deep breath before stepping out the car. The sun is shining as a group of stay-at-home moms pass by jogging while pushing their babies in strollers. It is a beautiful day.

The receptionist greeted me with a warm smile.

"Good morning, Drea. How are you?" "I'm doing good."

"I have you all checked in, and Dr. E will be out shortly." Mama and I both sit on the plush yellow sofa.

"This place is more of a teenager's room rather than a psychologist office," Mama leaned over and whispered.

"I know, right? It's not stuffy at all. Very warm."

"Minus Dr. E." Mama laughs. "She looks like a rock band groupie."

I scrunch up my face because I do not know if Mama is being shady toward Dr. E.

"I think she's a cool doctor, not like the typical ones."

"Hello, Drea." Dr. E says, walking out. She is sporting a peplum dress and has rings on each finger. Today, she swapped the Doc Martins for peep-toe heels, revealing an eagle tattoo on her right foot. "Hello, Mrs. Ramsey."

"Hello. And cute dress."

"Oh, thank you. One of my great finds from the thrift store." "Get out! Really?"

"Oh, yes. The thrift store is my jam."

"Huh. Well, I don't want to eat into Drea's session. I'll be out here waiting."

"We'll see you in a bit," Dr. E says as we disappear into her comfy office.

"Would you like something to drink before we get started?" "No, thanks."

"Okay, so first things first. How was the homework assignment?"

"It was harder than I thought. I struggled getting started."

"I know it can be tough writing down our feelings. Next time try freewriting."

"What is that?"

"In essence, it's about freeing yourself from any preconceived notions, attachments, or emotional investments that might limit your creative process. This is not an English paper you will turn in, and no one will ever read it unless you want them to. Just start writing without reading what you wrote down. When you're done or your hands get tired, simply stop and come back later to read what you wrote."

"That sounds simple enough."

"Yeah. Try it when you get back home." "Okay."

"So, let's switch gears for a moment. You mentioned last session that Daniel committed suicide because a video of him got out. Can you elaborate on that and what makes you think that could be linked to his suicide?"

"Wow." I clear my throat and rub my hands together. "I'm not sure if I'm ready to talk about it in detail. It's still too hard." I feel tears start to rush to my eyes.

On cue, Dr. E passes me some tissue. "Drea, its okay. We don't have to talk about it now if you don't want to.'

"Thank you for not forcing me to talk about it right now."

"I will never force you to talk about anything you're not comfortable talking about."

"So what should we talk about now?" I ask. "Whatever you want to talk about."

"I don't know."

"What about your panic attack at school? Or going to Daniel's funeral?"

"What about it?"

"Are you going?"

"Nah. I don't think so. Besides, most people are just going to be messy and nosey. I rather not see or be around that."

Dr. E doesn't respond immediately. I can see her thinking as she writes something down in her pink notepad. "Minus the people who are going there to be nosey, would you still like to go and pay your respects to one of your best friends?"

I shrug my shoulders. I'm not sure how I truly feel about going to Daniel's funeral. I never really thought about it. I'm still trying to process his death and write this ridiculous letter to a person who will never hear it. I feel my body get warm all over. My heart is starting to beat faster, and I can feel beads of sweat trickle down my back.

"Drea, are you okay?" Dr. E asks, looking concerned.

I couldn't speak. I just shook my head. Oh, not again. It's happening again. The same thing happened a couple of times at school after I heard about Daniel's suicide. It's like one minute I'm fine, and the next minute I've passed out and woke up in the nurse's office. What is wrong with me?

I can hear Dr. E voice trying to penetrate the static that's going on in my head. "Drea. Drea." She hurries to the table behind her desk where she has a mini fridge stocked with mini water bottles. "Drink this, Drea," she says, handing me a bottle of water.

I take a big gulp of it, and the coolness of the liquid streaming down my throat must have sent a signal to my brain because I slowly start to breath normally. My body temperature comes down, and I don't feel hot anymore.

I take another sip. "What just happened to me? I felt like that at school before."

"You were having a panic attack. How do you feel now?" "Okay, I guess. What caused it?"

"You tell me. We were discussing attending Daniel's funeral, and you started to become agitated."

I sit up in the chair, and I use my eyes to trace around Dr. E's face to see if she has an answer. "I'm not sure."

"Drea, it's okay if you're not ready to talk about a topic, but you have to communicate that and not hold it in. That sometimes may cause uninvited stressors into our lives and cause panic attacks. Do you understand?"

"Yeah, I think so."

"Let's stop here, and I'll see you day after tomorrow. On Friday."

"Okay."

Gathering up my belongings and feeling a little embarrassed, I walk toward the door.

"Oh, and Drea, in life we all face moments of difficulty and hardships that seem overwhelming. But ultimately, the only one who truly holds the key to overcome any obstacle is you, and it starts with compassion." She flashes half of a smile. "You will get through this, and your experiences will be able to help and teach others."

"Teach others what?"

"Remembering their own strength."

Her words are like puzzles I'm not sure how to piece together. But I know I can't keep living and reacting like this.

CHAPTER SIX

OCTOBER 2022

"Okay. Let's see if that works." Daniel eyes were steady on our ropeway project. "Damn. It's still not working."

"Maybe we should ask Mr. Fitzgerald. We've been stuck on this portion for a week now."

"No." There was a strict coldness in the sound of his voice.

"We can figure it out on our own."

Since we had been working together, I discovered that Daniel was not just fine. He was also kind and smart. We had a natural flow of conversation, and it felt like we had known each other for much longer than just a few weeks. It was like we were meant to meet, like the universe had conspired to bring us together. Looking back, I see the initial attraction I felt toward Daniel was just the start. As we spent more time together, I felt closer to him.

"Well, I really don't want to spend my whole Saturday at the library."

Since Daniel and I had been hanging out and working on our project, I'd become more comfortable with my voice. More specifically, more comfortable talking to my crush. He had not flirted with me or even made any cute remarks. I could not help but wonder if he really liked Paisley and was just working with me as a partner.

"Besides," I continued, "don't you have plans? I'm sure Paisley misses you."

"Me?" He almost looked offended by my question, "Why would Paisley have plans with me?"

"You two were buddy-buddy during the first week of school and I just thought . . . " I didn't finish my sentence. I felt like I was off with my questioning. Maybe we weren't as cool as I thought.

"Paisley is a cool classmate, and that's it."

"Okay. Sorry. No need to get mad."

"I'm not mad at you. I'm mad that we can't get this project to work."

Luckily, we reserved a private room in the library so we wouldn't be giving the rest of the library a show.

Silence filled the space between Daniel and me, and I played with my freshly-washed two-strand twist.

"Let's do something fun." Daniel turned to me with a goofy smile.

" Like what?"

"Let's go to the mall!"

"The mall? How are we gonna get there, and I don't have any money."

"Yeah, I guess you're right. Back in Elkhorn, the town was so small you could walk to get anywhere within ten minutes."

I played with one of my twists and thought of a better alternative than spending my Saturday at a library. "Your mom home?" He perked up again. "No, she's at work as usual."

"We can go back to your house and maybe have a fresh perspective on our project."

Is he really asking me to go back to my house? Did I just win the lottery without playing?

"Okay. We've stayed in here way too long."

Walking back to my house, my nerves were getting the best of me, and I become self-conscious all over again. Is my face super oily? Are my twists getting frizzy? One of the most noticeable effects of Coral Bluff's humidity was on my hair. As someone with naturally four-c hair, I had always had to be careful about how I styled and managed my curls. However, during the summer months, it seemed like no amount of effort could keep my hair under control. The humidity caused my curls to become frizzy and unruly, making it almost impossible to maintain any kind of hairstyle. This is why I usually opted for a two-strand twist; it lasted longer. But one would think it would get better as the season changed. And although the beautiful leaves were already changing, the humidity was still out to get me.

I felt butterflies and nerves in my stomach. This feeling was all too familiar as I walked up the steps of my porch. I was excited to walk into my home with Daniel. However, what I believed to be harmless emotions were actually deadly, stinky farts. Embarrassed and horrified in that very moment, I wish I had Harmony and Noelle here to help me and reassure me that everything was going to be fine.

"Drea, are you okay?" Daniel asked, walking too close for my comfort. I would just die if he smelt the funk that came out of me.

"Yeah, I'm good." I shuffled to the bathroom with my phone in my hand. "I'll be right back. Make yourself comfortable."

I closed the bathroom door without giving Daniel a chance to respond. I really couldn't believe this was happening to me. I never thought I would be in a situation like this, facing something that seemed completely unreal. Life could be so unpredictable. But some things are simply beyond our imaginations and expectations. And that's exactly where I found myself.

With tears starting to form in my eyes, and my insides being released in the toilet, I opened my phone, preparing to text the girls on our group.

Help. I need advice.

I saw the typing bubbles pop up.

What's up? Noelle responded back first, which was surprising because she was usually shopping or having some type of self-care day with her mom on the weekends.

I'm with Daniel at my house, and I have the bubble guts. I ended with the emoji of the girl's hand to her face.

Where is Daniel?

I don't know. I just ran to the bathroom.

Do this. Walk out and act like nothing even happened.

What?

Don't acknowledge what just happened. Act normal like you just had to check your makeup or something.

But I don't wear makeup.

LOL. I know. I'm just giving an example.

So don't mention how embarrassed I feel or explain my stomach?

Hell naw! Do you have body spray in the bathroom? Yeah.

Run the faucet and then flush so he won't hear the toilet.

After you wash your hands, spray yourself with the body spray but don't overdo it.

Got it! Whew!

Noelle ends our message with the fingers crossed emoji.

Lacking experience in the boys' department, I did exactly what Noelle said to do.

Coming out of the bathroom after what seemed to be an hour

later, I started to walk to the living room, thinking he would be waiting for me on the sofa. But I had to pass my room to get to the living room.

And I couldn't unsee what I saw next.

I stood in the doorway of my bedroom, my eyes widened in confusion.

Daniel, my crush, was going through my closet and singing softly with a high-pitch voice. My initial reaction was one of shock and disbelief. Was this some kind of prank? Had I entered an alternate reality? I stood frozen, trying to process what was happening in front of me. It was like I was watching a scene from a bizarre reality show. But as I continued to watch him, it became clear that this was not a joke. He was genuinely playing with my clothes and singing some pop song that I could not even recognize. And the way he sang, with exaggerated movements and facial expressions, it was clear that he was enjoying himself.

In that moment, I felt a mix of emotions. Part of me was amused by this unexpected turn of events. As I watched him continue to put on a show, my mind raced with questions. What made him do this? How long was I really in the bathroom for him to

go through my stuff? Was he trying to make fun of my clothes? Or was this just a random act of silliness? I couldn't come up with any logical explanation for his behavior.

"What are you doing?" I finally asked.

Daniel stopped singing and turned toward me with an expression of mistrust and nervousness.

Quickly putting back my clothes and straightening up the pile of shirts he placed on the bed, all he offered was "I'm sorry."

I couldn't believe it. I had never seen him like this before. He was always composed and collected, the one who seemed to have everything under control. And yet, in that moment, he appeared vulnerable and almost human. It was almost as if I were seeing a different side of him, one that he had kept hidden from the world until now.

I wondered what had caused this sudden change in him. Surely, the plain clothes in my closet could not have upset him. They could not have disrupted his calm demeanor. The questions swirled around in my mind, but I didn't know how to ask.

"Why were you playing in my closet?"

"Look, I'm sorry. I made a huge mistake, and I have to go."

"Now? We haven't finished our project. It's due in three weeks."

Not responding to my question, he quickly moved pass me walking toward the front door.

"Daniel, what's wrong?"

"Nothing, Drea, I just have to go. We'll catch up later." "And what about our project?"

"Don't worry about it. We still have time."

After following behind him as he walked out, I stood on the porch, watching his figure grow smaller in the distance. I felt a sense of fear creep in. Fear of the unknown. Fear of losing him. Fear of never being able to make things right again. I watched as he turned the corner and disappeared. The weight of the situation finally hit me, and I sank down onto the porch steps, my head in my hands.

Tears began to stream down my face as I thought about what this could mean for what I was trying to build with him. Memories from earlier in the day flashed through my mind like an IG reel. And now I was left alone on the front porch, trying to make sense of it all. I wiped away my tears and stood up, my body shaking with emotions of nervousness and anxiousness.

Does he hate me? Will we talk before our project is due? I wasn't sure what would happen next, but I definitely didn't expect today to end like this.

CHAPTER SEVEN

Monday was nothing short of dreadful. As I made my way to my seat in homeroom, I could not help but feel a heavy pit in my stomach. It was as if the weight of the world were resting upon my shoulders, and I could not shake off the feeling. I walked into the classroom and made eye contact with Daniel, hoping for a glimmer of acknowledgement or a simple smile. But to my surprise, he turned his head as if he did not even know who I was. And just like that, he started talking to Paisley, completely brushing me off. The sight of them conversing so casually sent a surge of pain through my heart. It was a sharp reminder of the reality I was facing: Daniel was mad at me, and I still did not know why.

"How was your weekend?" I heard Daniel ask Paisley as he chose the seat next to hers.

"Oh you know nothing special. Went shopping for dresses," she said with a devilish smirk on her face.

I could not stand her or this whole confusing situation. It wasn't just the fact that he seemed to have forgotten about me that hurt. It was the way he turned his back on me, as if our past friendship meant nothing to him. Since the day Mr. Fitzgerald partnered us up, we had been together every single day after school and on weekends. I wondered what happened to the Daniel I once knew. The one who used to make me laugh and feel understood. The way things had turned out between us felt like a cruel joke, and we still had to complete our project.

"I can't wait for you to see my dress at the dance," she continued as she rubbed his hand. "Do you have a date for the dance?"

Looking cool and collected as he always did, except for last Saturday in my bedroom, Daniel said, "No, I wasn't planning on going."

"Oh, you should. Our Homecoming dance is the biggest dance of the school year."

Daniel didn't answer right away. He finally responded, "Okay. Why not? I'll go."

"With me?"

"What do you mean?"

"Will you go to the dance with me?" Paisley almost looked annoyed, like she was trying to explain a difficult concept to him.

"Okay."

"Great. I'll call you this evening after cheer practice."

Overhearing their conversation made my skin itch. His hypocrisy was disgusting and was probably giving me a skin rash. Daniel literally told me he was not interested in her, and now they were making plans to go to the dance together. It was frustrating to see this kind of behavior from someone who was supposed to be a friend. It was disheartening to witness the disregard for others. I tried to tune them out for the remainder of class.

I could not get out of homeroom fast enough. The five- minute break between the next class was a great escape from the two of them. Is this what it's going to be like every day? Having to go back into class and seeing them laughing?

"There she is." Harmony said, pointing to me and walking with Noelle toward me in the hallway. "You ghosted us yesterday. We wanted to hear about your Saturday night with Daniel."

Harmony's question, mixed with her excitement, hit me like a bolt of lightning.

"Oh, it was cool."

"Wait. That's it? Your text read differently."

I had to see Daniel and Paisley flirt all day and explain to my friends what happened on Saturday when I was still trying to understand what happened.

"I had the bubble guts from the excitement, but Noelle told me what to do."

"Yeah, Drea, I was on the text too." Harmony and Noelle both laughed "And?" Noelle asked.

"And what?" I tried to play dumb.

Both were getting frustrated from my lack of details. Noelle asked, "What happened afterwards?"

"Oh, we ordered pizza and worked on our science project." I didn't know why I lied. These were my two besets friends in the world, and I lied to them about a boy who was not even talking to me. There was no real reason to lie except to protect my pride.

"Boring," Noelle said before pretending to yawn.

"And enough about me. What happened to you, Harmony? You didn't even respond," I asked, looking at Harmony and getting out of their line of questions.

"Matthew had a fever so Granny and I spent most of Saturday trying to break it.

Ring.

"Crap. That's the late bell. I'll see y'all later," I said, hurrying off to science class.

I was the last student walking into class, and Mr. Fitzgerald said, "Alright. I know this is Homecoming week and everyone is excited, but we are getting closer to you all's projects due date."

I swallowed a big lump of salvia. My nerves were getting the best of me.

"So for the remainder of our classes, I want everyone to work with their partners. Presentations begin the first Monday in December. I will have the order of presenting groups by tomorrow."

People started moving to different tables with their partners.

I didn't move. I couldn't move. I didn't know why, but I was glad Daniel had enough strength to come to my table.

"Hi," he said, sitting down.

"Hi."

"I think I figured out why the ropeway wouldn't work. We have faulty wires. I didn't notice it before, but there's a small tear in one of the wires. My mom is taking me to Target after school today to get a new set."

He's talking like nothing happened two days ago. Does he not understand the gravity of confusion and hurt he's caused me? Am I tripping?

But all I offered was, "Okay."

"The only thing left is to finish the research paper. Can you work on that?"

"Sure."

I could hear all the groups talking around us as we sat in silence. My only comfort was the project was almost done and we didn't ever have to speak to each other ever again. We did not say anything else to each other for the rest of class.

As Monday morning turned into Monday afternoon, the last bell rung, and I could not wait to go home. At least there I could be with my thoughts without being interrupted.

Being alone had been something that I had made peace with since Mama and Daddy's divorce. The peace and quiet, the ability to be lost in my own thoughts without any interruptions, had become valuable to me. And after the day I had, I needed it. So when Noelle told me she had cheer practice after school and Harmony had to leave early to care for Matthew while her Granny went to the doctor, I was excited to walk home alone.

However, my moment of solitude was short-lived when Oliver suddenly appeared before I could get off the school's grounds. My initial reaction was one of annoyance. What was he doing here? Didn't he have anything better to do than bother me on my walk home? It seemed that no matter how many times I made it clear that I wanted to be alone, Oliver always managed to find a way to insert himself into my life. And every time this happened, I found myself feeling more and more annoyed. But at the same time, I could not bring myself to completely shut him out. I had known Oliver since we were kids, and both of us had been through so much. The same year my parents divorced was the same year his baby sister drowned in their swimming pool. No one knew how to deal with a divorce or a death, but we never talked about it.

"Wait up. Why are you walking so fast, Drea?" he said, jogging to catch up.

"I'm just ready to get home."

"It's good to finally see you alone."

"The girls had other plans."

"I mean from your boyfriend Daniel." He stopped and made sure his words land perfectly on my ear drums.

"Daniel is not my boyfriend. We are science partners." As I said my words, I felt a shiver run down my back. They seemed to have a power of their own, one that I wasn't sure I was ready to accept. My words shook me to the core in a way I had never experienced before.

"Oh."

"Yeah. So stop assuming."

As Oliver walked beside me now, making small talk and joking around like everything was normal, I still felt conflicted. The realization of my words made me sad.

"Do you have any plans for homecoming this weekend?" "Not really."

"You're not going to the game or the dance?"

"I haven't gotten a dress or anything so probably not." "I know Noelle will be there."

"She has to be there. She's a cheerleader, silly." "What about Harmony?"

"I don't know. I haven't asked her."

"Well, I'm going."

"Good for you, Oliver." I could see my house coming up, and I increased my speed so I could finish our conversation more quickly.

"Will you be my date to the Homecoming dance?"

I stopped and was forced to abandon my idea of escaping Oliver's conversation.

"What?"

"I want you to go with me to the dance."

"Didn't you just hear me say I don't have a dress?"

"It's only Monday, and the dance isn't till Saturday. I know you'll find something. Besides, it's not like we have to match. This isn't prom."

"I don't know, Oliver."

"Oh, come on, Drea. You know our families will support it.

Your dad always liked me."

He knew bringing my daddy into the conversation would force my decision. My father had always held a special place in my heart. I was a daddy's girl through and through, and my love for him never faded, even when he moved back to Chicago after the

divorce. He was my hero, my protector, and my role model.

I knew Oliver was right. Daddy always liked Oliver's quirky, nonconforming personality. I remembered when I started middle school, some of the boys in my class started smoking. They would hide behind the school building during lunch breaks and smoke their vape pens. As a twelve-year-old, I didn't understand why they were doing it. But I soon realized it was because they thought it made them look cool. However, not all the boys were doing it. Oliver was not trying to fit in or look cool with his uneven caramel brown skin tone and thick, black glasses. Instead, he stayed true to himself, even if it meant standing out from the crowd. Oliver was and always had been comfortable in his own skin.

I took a deep breath of the warm fall air and said, "Okay." "Yeah?" "Yeah."

Pulling me in unexpectedly, Oliver hugged me so tight I felt like I was going to burst into a million pieces. I was shocked by his gesture, but I secretly felt happy for being wanted. I mean, Daniel hasn't talked to me for real. Plus, he was going to the dance with Ms. Paisley.

"You've made my day, Drea." Grinning like a child going to Walt Disney World for the first time, Oliver spun me around. "Okay. Okay, Oliver. Calm down," I said, now laughing. "Now can I get your number? I'll text you a picture of my suit when I get home."

"I thought you said we didn't have to match." "We don't, but you can use it for reference."

"Sure, why not? Give me your phone." I typed in my number and saved it under Drea.

"Great. I'll text you. See you later." "Bye."

Walking up the porch to my house, I realized that maybe I was tripping over Daniel way too long. Instead of wondering why he had turned his back on me, I should have been asking why I was still holding on to someone who clearly didn't care about me or my feelings. It was a harsh reality to face, but I knew that I deserved better. I deserved someone who would stand by my side through thick and thin and not just walk away. Although, I did wonder what Daniel would say when he saw me with Oliver at the dance.

CHAPTER EIGHT

Last night, I did not sleep that well. It seemed like no matter how hard I tried, I could not get comfortable. I tossed and turned and ended up waking up at least twice throughout the night. I was too cold and then too hot. It was frustrating to say the least. But what was even more bizarre was the dream I had. Usually, I did not remember my dreams, but this one was so strange and intense that it stuck with me even after I woke up. It felt like I was in a movie or some alternate universe.

It was a beautiful spring day, and I was walking with Oliver.

He grabbed my hand and pulled me over onto the sidewalk. He looked deeply into my eyes and smiled before he gave me a kiss. Then, out of nowhere, the sun was eclipsed by something dark. It looked like a swarm of something heading straight toward me. It took me a while to figure out what this object was flying toward me until I realized they were black birds. There were thousands of them flying around me and Oliver. I tried to fan them off while covering my face. I noticed Oliver standing there, looking at me without a care in the world. I started screaming and panicking until Harmony and Noelle came out of nowhere and grabbed my arm. They pulled me into this abandoned building with water covered the floor. I could still hear the birds outside going crazy and wondered if Oliver were still outside.

Just as I was about to thank my besties for saving me, my four front teeth fell out. I was so embarrassed and confused. For a moment I stood there, holding my teeth, trying to understand what happened. Noelle and Harmony stared at me, not saying a word. I tried to run away, but the water on the floor was not water. It was some type of liquid glue that had me stuck. The more I tried to get out, the more the glue-like substance was pulling me back. I dropped my teeth and reached out toward Harmony and Noelle. Before I could make sense of it all, I woke up. It took me a few moments to realize that it was just a dream, but it left me feeling unsettled. The images and symbols in the dream seemed to have some deeper meaning, but I could not quite grasp it.

I knew it was not time for me to get up for school yet because it was still dark outside. Reaching for my phone from under my pillow, I checked the time: one thirty-three. I lay in bed, trying to fall back asleep, but I could not stop thinking about the dream. It

felt like a sign or a message, but I could not decipher it. Maybe it was my mind playing tricks on me, or maybe it was just a random jumble of thoughts and memories. Whatever the case may be, one thing was for sure: it was hard for me to go back to sleep.

I was already lying awake when my six o'clock alarm went off. Feeling groggy and a little anxious about my dream, I texted Auntie Jolie. She of all people could understand my dream. She not only studied astrology and numerology, but she could also decode dreams. I had even heard her talking to people who were not physically there before. And although I do not completely understand her world of mystics, I knew she would not judge me for my dream. In fact, she could tell me what the hell it meant.

Good morning. Are you up, Auntie?

Two minutes later, she responds: Grand Rising, niece. Yes, I'm up. Are you good?

Not really. Can you talk?

Before Auntie Jolie responded through text, she called me. "Is everything alright, Drea?"

"Yes, ma'am. I just had a crazy dream last night." "Oh, yeah? What about, sweetie?"

I told her about the dream, including the blackbirds, the girls saving me, my teeth falling out, and the glue on the floor. Auntie Jolie listened intently and was quiet for what seemed like a long time. I had to look at my phone to make sure we were not disconnected. Then she finally spoke, "I'm glad you reached out to me."

"Why? Is my dream bad?"

"I don't judge a dream good or bad, Drea. Dreams are messages from our subconscious and the Universe to give us messages we sometimes can't see."

"So what is the message of my crazy dream?" "I'd rather tell you in person."

"In person? Is it that bad?"

"Remember, it's not whether the dream is good or bad. It's the messages that is trying to come forth, and I rather interpret it in person." She paused for another minute and continued, "I'll head out in a couple hours and should be there by the time school is out."

"You're going to drive all the way from New Orleans to Coral Bluff to interpret a dream?"

"I'm driving the six hours to be with my niece and interpret your dream."

Feeling more anxious and confused, I hesitantly said,

"Okay."

"I love you, Drea."

The tone of her voice sounded so final it scared me a little. "Love you too, Auntie."

She hung up before I could ask any more questions. I lay in bed for a few more minutes. My pajamas had a slight odor and still a little damp from me sweating last night. My mouth was dry, and my thoughts were a little disoriented. There was not much time to reflect on my dream or restless night any longer; I had to get dressed for school.

I walked to school by myself. The girls did not text back this morning when I asked them if they were meeting at my house to walk to school. I assumed Noelle had to get to school earlier to prepare for our Homecoming game. And Harmony was probably staying home today with Matthew again.

I tried to distract myself as I walked down the street to school. I admired the beautiful southern sunrays kissing my forehead while the birds chirped in the background. Plus, I was still thinking about being asked to be Oliver's date.

By the time I reached school, all the thoughts that swirled around my head left little to no room to be distracted by Daniel and Paisley's kissy-face interactions during class. Before I knew it, school was over, and I couldn't be happier. My tiredness completely hit me by sixth period. So, by the time the last bell rang to go home, I didn't even stop by my locker. I rushed to the front entrance and picked up my pace as I walked home.

I was so ready to lay down in my cozy bed that I failed to notice the car in the driveway. A familiar scent filled my nose as I stepped into my house. It was a smoky, earthy aroma that instantly transported me to a place of calmness and relaxation. It was the scent of Palo Santo. The smell was both comforting and thoughtful, stirring up memories and emotions from my childhood.

I closed my eyes and took a deep breath, allowing the aroma to fill my lungs and calm my mind. The moment I smelled the familiar scent, I knew she was here.

With my eyes still closed, standing in the living room, I yelled out, "Auntie Jolie! Auntie, is that you?"

I could hear feet walking from the back of the house. And then she appeared.

"Hello, honey," she said, walking toward me with her arms stretched out.

My Auntie was gorgeous to me. Her short statue exaggerated her curves while exuding a confidence that demanded attention. Her hazel eyes were captivating and seemed to sparkle against her rich amber skin tone. Of course, she was wearing her signature black flowy dress paired with black lipstick on her full lips.

"You made it?"

"I told you I would be here before you got out of school."

She was a woman of few words, and sometimes spoke in riddles, but her presence spoke volumes. When I was younger, I remembered watching her in awe. She effortlessly solved crossword puzzles and could tell people their future by just looking at them.

Her love for literature was evident in her huge collection of books that lined the shelves of my grandparents' home in Louisiana. She had a deep interest in astrology and numerology, and her stories of ancient civilizations and cultures fascinated me.

"How did you get in?"

"You know I remember where your mother keeps the spare key. She's a creature of habit."

"How long are you staying?"

"Oh, I don't know, honey. Until it's time to go." "Are you cooking something?"

"You know I can't come in and not cook."

Growing up, I always had a special connection with my auntie. She was my mother's younger sister, but in many ways, she seemed to understand me more than my own mother. My auntie was a mysterious woman, with an air of intelligence and depth that drew me in. As I grew older, I realized that my admiration for her went beyond the surface. My auntie was not just my mother's sister; she was my confidante and friend.

"Let me guess, your infamous gumbo?"

"Yes, ma'am. And it's the perfect time now that it's fall."

"But it's still pretty warm outside."

"It doesn't matter, baby. You don't cook for the weather; you cook for the season."

"I'll wash my hands and help you."

"So how have you been? I mean, besides that wild dream."

"I'm good. This boy from school asked me to the winter dance this Saturday."

"And you're going?"

"Yes, but I don't have a dress yet. I just decided yesterday that I was going."

"I can take you dress shopping. We can go look for dresses tomorrow unless you want to wait for your mother."

"She doesn't stay home long enough to take me shopping so we can go tomorrow."

"She's still working those crazy hours?"

"Yeah, and when she's here, she just sleeps or watches television."

Auntie Jolie takes a deep breath and stir the gumbo before speaking. "You know, baby, life can be hard, and sometimes when things don't go the way you planned, it can be devastating. Your mama is just trying to find her way through this chaotic world."

"I don't know. I mean we don't even talk about Daddy, the divorce, or Franklin moving with Daddy. It's like nothing ever happened."

Auntie was silent for a moment but then broke her silence.

"Have you ever wanted something, maybe for your birthday or Christmas? You wanted it so badly you couldn't see yourself without it. But when your birthday came, you didn't get it?"

Auntie's question didn't make me think of a gift, but I thought of Daniel.

"Yes, I have."

"And how did it feel?"

"I felt disappointed and maybe I didn't deserve it." I can feel my eyes getting watery.

Auntie Jolie comes over and hugged me. "Give your mama more time, baby. Everyone's healing journey is different."

"And mine? When is my healing going to come?" "You're healing now, baby. You may not see it, but your

strength is what sets you apart from a lot of people. Trust your strength and the process. That was also what your dream was trying to tell you."

Her advice was always wise, and she never judged me for my mistakes. My auntie was a great listener, and her empathy and compassion made me feel understood and accepted.

"Now set the table so we can eat," she continued as she wiped away my tears.

Placing the deep yellow and blue bowls on the table, I used my strength to ask the question I have not been able to ask aloud: "How do I get a boy to like me?"

Auntie Jolie turned from the stove and placed one hand on her hips. "From what I'm hearing, you don't need to convince that boy to like you. He's completely into you."

"No, not Oliver. Another boy."

"Oh. Another boy, huh? Why, Drea, I didn't think you were boy crazy.

"No. No. No. It's not like that. This boy transferred to our school at the beginning of the year, and we are both in the same classes. He is so fine. We were paired up to be science partners. He came over on Saturday, and I caught him playing in my clothes, but when I asked him about it, he got mad and left. Now he's not talking to me anymore."

Silence filled the room again. Auntie Jolie motion to bring over the bowls. "You know, baby, there's no guaranteed formula for making someone like you. And sometimes it takes a person a while to understand what he or she wants."

"So, what should I do?"

"Nothing."

"Nothing?"

"That's right. Nothing. In due time, you will see that he needs time to understand and decide what he wants."

Blowing the hot gumbo, I scooped up a piece of Conecuh sausages and shrimp. "How much time should I give him?"

"As much time as he needs." Blowing on her spoon, she continued, "The journey of self-discovery is one that is crucial for each person's personal growth. So, give him time. Remember your dream was telling you to trust the process."

"I hope you're right."

A sly giggle was the only response she offered as we continued to eat our gumbo.

After dinner, I cleaned the kitchen and put away the dishes. I saw Auntie Jolie casually walk toward Franklin's old room. It had been empty since he moved out with daddy, but my auntie always seemed to gravitate toward that space. I could not blame her though because it was such a cozy and inviting room. Just as I finished wiping down the counter, my phone started ringing. I checked the caller ID and saw that it was my dad FaceTiming me. Smiling, I answered the call and could immediately see his face on the screen.

"Hey, kiddo!" Daddy said, putting up the phone close to his face, showing the stubble of gray hairs in his beard. Everyone said I looked like him. We shared the same oval-shaped face, deep brown complexion, and almond-shaped eyes. I was his twin.

Putting down the dry cloth and walking back to my room, I was so excited to talk to him. "Hey, Daddy. What are you doing?" "Oh, just finishing up grading some papers. Taking a break now before I get ready for bed."

Daddy was a high school math teacher and had a way of explaining complex equations in a simple and easy-to-understand manner. Other kids complained about math being their least favorite subject. I could not wait to come home and share with my dad the new things I had learned in school. My mom used to say that my love for numbers came from my dad. When I was younger, I would sit next to him at the kitchen table while he graded his students' homework and tests. I was fascinated by the way he was able to solve problems quickly and effortlessly without an answer key. He would often challenge me with puzzles and math problems to sharpen my math skills. Looking back, I realize that he was teaching me without me realizing it. My dad's teaching style was not just limited to the classroom. He would often use real-life scenarios to explain mathematical concepts to me. For example, when I was learning about percentages, he used our weekly grocery trips to show me how to calculate discounts and savings.

"I just finished cleaning the kitchen. Auntie Jolie cooked her famous gumbo."

"Aunt Jolie is there? Tell her I said hello." "I will. How's Franklin and Grandma?"

"Everyone is doing well, or as well as you can expect."

The tone of his voice changed when he answered, and I knew it was because of Franklin. My brother was always in and out of trouble and had a hard time following the rules. As we got older and our parents went through their divorce, it was clear that my brother needed a strong male figure in his life. Well, that was what I overheard Mama tell someone on the phone one day. So, it was decided by both my parents that Franklin would go with our daddy.

"I'm counting down the days when I get to see you all over the Christmas break."

"I can't wait. I already got your ticket."

"How long will I be there?"

"Two weeks, your entire winter break." "Perfect! I wish I could stay longer."

Laughing, he said, "Why? It's bitterly cold and snowy up here. You have warm weather down there in Alabama."

"But I don't mind the snow. I think it's pretty."

"We'll see. How was school today? And how's that science project going?"

"School was okay, and the science project isn't finished yet." "What's the hold up? Didn't you tell me it was due by the first of December?"

"Yeah, but me and my partner got into a fight this past weekend and now we are not talking."

Daddy adjusted himself on the sofa. "Drea, you know this project is fifty percent of your grade, so I highly suggest that you work through whatever problem you and the partner have and complete this project. What's more important: your pride or your grades?"

"I know, Daddy. I'll figure it out."

"I know you will. You are the smartest tenth grader I know."

Both laughing and lightening up the mood, I said, "Guess what?"

"What?"

"Oliver asked me to go to our Homecoming dance this Saturday."

"I've always liked that Oliver boy. He's a good and respectable young man."

"Yeah, I know you've always liked him. Auntie Jolie is taking me dress shopping after school tomorrow."

"Send me a picture of the dress you decide. Nothing too short or tight."

"Oh, Daddy, I know."

"Look, I know how teenage boys think." "I promise I'll show you the dress." "Well, I'm about to get ready for bed." "Yeah, me too."

"I love you, kiddo, and I'll call tomorrow." "Love you too, Daddy."

Despite all the changes from the divorce, one thing remained constant: my love for my daddy. He had always been there for me, supporting me through every milestone and hard time. He might not physically be present every day now, but his love and guidance were always with me.

CHAPTER NINE

The next few days were full of dress shopping, hair and makeup sessions, and occasional check-ins with Daniel at school for our project. I didn't think about Daniel as much over the week. His presence with Paisley in class did not annoy me as much either. I guess my attention was consumed with girlie stuff, but I kind of liked it.

As promised, Auntie Jolie made it her mission to find me the perfect dress. After school, we went to boutiques and department stores, trying on dresses of all styles and colors. It was intimidating at times, but we were determined to find one that would make me feel confident and beautiful. After a couple of days of trying on dresses, I finally found the perfect one. It was a delicate, yellow, knee-length dress with intricate beading around the chest and a touch of lace on the sleeves. As I twirled around in front of the mirror, I felt like a princess. Auntie Jolie had spotted the dress on the sales rack between hundreds of dresses I would not dare tackle. It was like the dress was waiting for us to find it and make it my own.

And just when I thought the hard part was over, the hairstyle options were next. We tried different looks: updos, half- up/half-down, and even wearing my natural curly afro. Then, we picked a style that would match my dress and the look I was going for.

And through all the commotion of preparing for the dance in less than a week, I still had to focus on other responsibilities, one of them being my school project with Daniel. Even though we still were not cool, we made sure to have occasional check-ins at school to finalize our project.

Saturday finally arrived, and I could not contain my excitement. Harmony was not going because she wanted to be with her baby. Noelle was going, but I am quite sure she will leave early with some of the upper-class students from the cheer squad. I was not as popular as Noelle, so the invites usually skipped me. But tonight would be me and Oliver.

As I slipped on my dress, I felt like a million bucks. The color was vibrant, and the fabric was soft against my skin. It hugged my petite figure in all the right places, emphasizing my curves and making me feel confident. I could not have done it without my auntie. She had been excited to help me get ready for the event and even Mama took off to see me.

We talked about Mama and Auntie Jolie's high school dance stories while Auntie worked her magic on my hair. She made it into an elegant crown braid with a few curls falling down my face. I could not believe how beautiful the hairstyle looked on me. It was a work of art with every strand carefully placed and secured with bobby pins. My auntie had a way of making even the simplest hairstyles look stunning. With my hair done and my dress on, I took one last look in the mirror before I FaceTimed daddy.

I couldn't stop smiling at the sight of myself and my dad's reaction confirmed my opinion.

"Wow. You look beautiful. I can't call you my kiddo anymore."

"Aww, Daddy, I will always be your kiddo."

"Nah, you're my princess." Blushing, I heard the doorbell ring.

"Daddy, I have to go, I think Oliver is here."

"Okay. Have fun and be safe. Text me when you get back in the house."

"I will. Love you."

"Love you too."

After one more look in the mirror, I whispered, "You got this, Drea."

Picking up my phone, I walked toward the living room where Mama had already opened the door for Oliver.

"Wow," Oliver said as I made my way toward him. "You look amazing, Drea."

Mama and Auntie Jolie were smiling ear to ear, watching us through their phone while taking pictures.

"Thank you. You don't look bad yourself." And I wasn't lying. I had known Oliver a long time and had never seen him anything other than annoying. But tonight was different. He was different. He even looked taller than me. I could not help but sigh as I admired his dark gray suit. He was effortlessly dressed. The off- white shirt he wore, with its crisp collar and neatly pressed sleeves, was the perfect complement to the suit. But it was the touch of yellow in his pocket square that reassured me my dress was meant for me. It added just the right pop of color, making him stand out in a sea of boring dark suits.

"You two stand right here and let me take a few more pictures." I hadn't seen Mama this happy in a long time. Her smile made me feel like she was truly proud of me.

And after a thousand pictures, we made our way to the car where his mom was waiting to drop us off. Stepping into the baby- powder-scented car, I slid over to let Oliver in.

"Hello, Mrs. Greene."

"Hey, Drea. You look so beautiful."

"Thank you."

"This will obviously be a quick drive, but I wasn't going to have y'all walking down the street in y'all fancy clothes."

"We definitely appreciate it."

When we pulled up to the school's gym, Oliver stepped out first and turned around to grab my hand.

"You don't mind if we hold hands so we don't lose each other?"

I was taken back. I have never kissed, let alone held a boy's hand before. But it felt right, and I held his hand back.

We walked into the winter-wonderland-themed gym. The transformation was surprising. What was once an uninviting space had been turned into a magical icy paradise. The blues and silver that adorned the walls and floors, along with the sparkling lights and decorations, created an atmosphere that was both enchanting and surreal. The familiar basketball hoops and bleachers were replaced by towering ice sculptures and intricate snowflake designs. The floor, now covered in glistening white material, resembled freshly fallen snow, which invited us to leave our footprints on it. It was hard to believe that this was the same gym where we had PE.

The attention to detail was evident in every aspect of the transformation. Even the ceiling was decorated with cascading icicles, giving the illusion of being inside an ice castle. The walls were draped with luxurious blue and silver fabrics, adding a touch of elegance to the space.

"You want something to drink?"

"Nah, not right now."

"You want to dance?"

"Dance? Um, not right now." I'd never danced in public; I did not even know if I were a good dancer.

"What do you want to do?"

Before I could answer, I saw Noelle heading straight toward me.

"Damn, Drea, that's you? I had to see this masterpiece up close."

"Shut up, Noelle."

"No, seriously, you look good girl. Doesn't she look good?" she asked Oliver.

"Yes, she looks very good."

I turned to him as he emphasized the very while licking his lips.

"Who are you here with?"

"It's a group of us, mostly the cheerleaders." "Paisley with y'all?"

"Girl, nah. You know I don't fool with her like that."

She must have come with Daniel, but I had not seen either one of them yet. Maybe he changed his mind.

"I'll catch you later. Oliver, you better take care of my bestie."

And just like that, Noelle disappeared into the crowd. Song after song, the DJ was hitting. Between the ambiance of the decor and the music, I could feel myself getting lost in the beats. Every note, every beat, was resonating with my very being. I started to move my shoulders. Suddenly, I felt Oliver's eyes piercing me. A small smirk appeared on his lips, and I could feel my cheeks flush with heat.

"What?"

"I see you're feeling this song. Are you sure you don't want to dance?"

"Positive."

He took me by the hand again and said, "Come with me." "Where are we going?" I asked the back of him.

"Just trust me."

We walked out of the gym and ended up in a small hallway separating the girls' and boys' locker room.

"What are we doing here? We are missing the party."

"I couldn't really talk to you in there; the music was too loud."

"Well, what do you need tell me?"

He paused for a minute, looking down at his shoes, before he said, "I really like you, Drea."

I didn't say anything. I would not have predicted that this was what he wanted to talk to me about.

"And when I saw you come out of your room tonight, I knew."

"Knew what?"

"I had to kiss you."

He lifted his head and stared into my eyes. Without breaking eye contact, he started moving toward me. His steps were confident, and he moved with a fluid grace that was as thrilling as his gaze. My heart started racing, and I bit my lip in anticipation.

It happened so fast, and yet it felt like time stood still. It was just a quick kiss, but it left me stunned, and I wanted more. I could feel my heart racing as I tried to process what had just happened. I was caught off guard by the first kiss; it was unexpected and yet so electric. But it was the second kiss that really got me. It was intentional, slow, and definitely sexy. As our lips met again, I could feel the intensity between us. His hand gently cupped my face as he deepened the kiss. It was like he was exploring every inch of my lips, savoring every moment. I could feel myself getting lost in passion and desire. I felt like we were the main characters in a romance novel. Time seemed to slow down as we continued to kiss; each caress of his lips against mine sent shivers down my spine. I almost forgot he had braces as they did not stand in the way. I could not help but melt into him, my body responding to his touch in ways I never thought possible. As we finally broke apart, we were both left breathless and wanting more.

Our eyes locked, and I could see the desire in his eyes. It was clear that this was not just a brief moment, but something that has been developing over the years. That simple, slow, and sexy kiss had awakened something inside of me. My first kiss left me feeling like a fire had ignited. In that moment, it became clear to me that there was no force more powerful than a kiss. It could captivate, connect, and create an unbreakable bond between two people.

"Drea, are you okay?"

I was still mesmerized by that unforgettable second kiss.

And as I stood, lost in my thoughts, I couldn't help but smile. "I'm good. I think I may need that cup of punch now." "Okay, let's get you that drink."

Going back to the gym, I could feel the electricity between us, and a rush of excitement coursed through my veins. The flirtatious tone of his voice becomes more evident as he whispered in my ear, "I'll be back," making my heart race even faster.

I found an empty table and made my way to it. The punch line was wrapped around the gym so I knew he would be a while. I readjust my dress and watched familiar faces dance to all the top-twenty songs while singing along to it. Until my eyes caught him.

My daddy always said that clothes made the man, and in the case of Daniel, that statement could not be truer. Walking into the room in his blue suit and black button-down shirt, he exuded a certain aura of sophistication and confidence. The blue color of his suit was unlike any I had ever seen before. It was a deep shade of blue that seemed to change in the light, giving it an almost mystical quality. The fabric looked smooth, and with every step, it moved gracefully with him. It was clear that this was not your average off- the-rack suit. But it was not just the suit that took my breath away. It was the black button-down shirt he wore underneath it. The plain contrast between the blue suit and the black shirt created an amazing image that made him look like a spy straight out of a James Bond movie. The shirt itself was tailored, hugging his frame in all the right places and showing off his toned body.

What was I doing? I literally just had my first kiss with the only boy who has always been nice and respectable to me. And within minutes apart, I saw Daniel, and I fell back under his spell. Was my auntie right? Was I boy crazy?

As I looked at him, I could not help but admire how good he looked. It was not just about his appearance, but the way he carried himself added to his overall appeal. He stood tall and confident, as if he knew the effect he had on others. He had a certain charm and charisma that drew people in and made them want to be around him. It was as if he had a secret that only he knew and everyone else wanted to uncover.

Paisley wasn't too far behind. She was trying to hang onto his arm, but it seemed as if he was purposely trying to break away from her. But she did not look like she minded. She was more concerned with her friends idolizing and adoring her outfit. Daniel was clearly just an accessory to her.

The room was filled with the buzz of conversations and laughter, but my eyes were still drawn to him. He stood across the room, his tall frame towering over the others, and our eyes met. It was as if we were communicating with each other without a single word being said. I looked away, feeling embarrassed that he seen me staring at him. But I could not look anywhere else, my eyes were drawn to him. I felt a flutter of excitement in my stomach.

When our eyes locked again, he slowly motioned toward the hallway, his lips forming a sly smile. My heart skipped a beat. Was he signaling me to follow him? Was this some kind of game? But without hesitation, I made my way toward the hallway, where he was waiting for me. Just moments before, I was in this very spot where I had my first kiss. Would there be another kiss from Daniel?

It was almost like we were in our own little world, separated from the chaos of the party. As I walked closer, I took in his features. His smile was contagious, and I found myself smiling back at him without even realizing it. His eyes sparkled as he looked at me, and I could not deny the chemistry between us.

"You are serving it, Drea."

"Aww, thank you. You look very nice too."

"Thanks. This may be my favorite suit. It makes me feel like a real man."

"Well, it looks good on you."

Awkward silence nudged itself in between us.

"Look, I wanted to apologize for how I behaved at your house last Saturday. I shouldn't have touched your things."

"I didn't care you were touching my clothes. I was confused as to why you left so quickly and have been giving me the cold shoulder all week."

"Yeah."

"It really hurt my feelings, Daniel, and I thought we were better than that." There. I finally said it. I wish I could say more, but I needed him to know that my feelings were hurt, and he was the one who did it.

"Drea, I really admire you. You are smart, thoughtful, and have an innocence that is not like most people. I love that about you. And I am so sorry for hurting your feelings."

I could not help but blush. His words were honest and healing to me. Now with a newfound spirit of confidence, I made the space between us smaller.

"Thank you for your words." I took his hand. They looked so masculine, but they were soft.

"Drea, what are you doing?"

"I think I'm about to kiss you."

Taking his hand back, he stepped away from me. Did I misread his intentions? I felt exposed, humiliated, and now angry.

"So why did you call me out here?"

"To apologize for my behavior and . . . "

"And what?" I could feel myself getting more and more impatient with him playing with my emotions. "Is it Paisley?"

"What? No."

"Then what is it, Daniel?" "I'm gay."

At first, his words did not register with me. But as his words sank in, they hit me like a ton of bricks. My mind suddenly became a whirlwind of questions and fears. I felt like I was suffocating under the weight of my own thoughts. Daniel was searching for a response, but his words were now just a blur in the background. I could not even begin to comprehend what I was feeling and hearing. All I could hear was the loud pounding of my heart and the sound of my own thoughts racing. Suddenly, I broke through the silence, "I gotta go."

"Drea, wait. Please."

But his pleas fell on deaf ears because I ran back into the gym. I met Oliver back at the once-empty table where there were now two other couples from the eleventh grade.

"Where did you go?"

"I just needed some fresh air." "You okay?"

I could feel the tears trying to form in my eyes, but I kept fighting them. "No, I'm not okay. Can we go?"

"Sure, I can call my mom."

"No, we can walk back to my house, and you can have her pick you up there. I just need to leave now."

"Wow, that kiss really did something to you, huh? There's no better time than to ask now."

"Ask what?"

"Drea, will you be my girlfriend?"

"What?"

"Will you be my girlfriend?"

I could not hold in my emotions of anger and uneasiness any longer. No matter how much I wanted to be strong, to push through the pain and keep a brave face, I could not do it anymore. The wall I had built around myself was crumbling, and there was nothing I could do to stop it. I could feel my body shaking as I gave in to my tears and let them consume me. All the hurt, anger, and confusion that I had been holding back came rushing out in an unstoppable flood. My mind was a jumbled mess of thoughts and feelings, and I couldn't make sense of any of it.

Chapter Ten

Present Day

I can hear Daniel now: "I'm too big for this city. You have to be a certain way to show your manhood, and I'm tired of living my life in a box." He would be right. I wish he were here to say it from his own mouth, and I wouldn't be stuck with the task of writing to a dead friend.

It's a strange feeling, not knowing what to write. I'm at a loss for words. As I sit here, staring at a blank page, I realize that even if Daniel were standing in front of me right now, I wouldn't know what I would say to him.

Daniel was always the talkative one between us. He never hesitated to start up a conversation with anyone, and his charm and charisma could light up any room. He had this infectious energy about him that drew people toward him. But now, as I struggle to find the right words to write, I realize that it's not just his absence that has left me speechless, but the weight of what he had to go throughout his life.

Plus, despite all these challenges, I have found myself withdrawing from the world. I feel like a hostage in my own room, unable to face the outside and the problems that come with it. It is easier to bury myself in my room and shut out the world than to confront the reality of my strained friendships and the loss of my friend.

Why? The world pushed Daniel to take his life.

I don't know why Dr. E gave me this stupid assignment anyway. I tap my pen against the wordless paper. Maybe there's nothing left to say. Our friendship has come to an end, and it was time to move on. Besides, why would I want bring back old memories and open up old wounds? And I'm sure I'm not ready for that.

So much has happened this school year, I'm not sure if I or any or my friendships can survive. It's funny because my weekends used to symbolize a brief false sense of freedom away from school. Harmony, Noelle, and I used weekends during second semester to reset, have fun, and count down the weeks left to summer break.

Today, I am sitting in my room, looking out at the shining sun, and realize that the week at home has gone by in a blur. It is amazing how the beautiful rays of sunlight can make everyone want to step outside and enjoy the day. Unfortunately, I have been cocooned in my room, disconnected from the outside world, since the news of Daniel. I have not returned any calls or texts; barely spoken to my family; and only left my room to grab a quick bite to eat, use the bathroom, and go to my counseling appointments. It is not like me to be this introverted and secluded. But when I think about Daniel or my family trying to talk about it, I become overwhelmed and retreat for more alone time.

Looking out the window, I see people enjoying the outdoors and connecting with loved ones, and I cannot help but feel a little left out. I wish I had the strength to go outside and enjoy the beautiful weather. Or even hangout with the girls or Oliver. But as of now, I need a little break from the chaos. My mind is flooded with the memory of Daniel, and my heart is broken from losing a great friend.

The only person who seems to think I'm getting better is Dr. E. But maybe I am making progress. This is the first time this week I have had my curtains drawn back to get natural sunlight. Now sitting at my desk, I am trying to further my progress.

Let me try this free writing foolishness she told me about.

Putting pen to paper, I start writing without thinking. But just as I am getting into the flow of writing, I am interrupted with voices outside my door. The familiar voices of Mama and Auntie Jolie talking to someone drift to my room from the living room. I quickly place my pen down and turn away from the window to make sure my bedroom door is closed. I do not want to be disturbed.

The sound of approaching footsteps causes my heart to race. I feel like I am in the movie Taken, and my first instinct is to hide. I take a deep breath and try to calm my nerves. I carefully press my hands together, not able to move from the window. And then a gentle knock greets me.

"Drea. honey, Harmony and Noelle are here. They want to see you."

I do not respond, but I can hear her say, "Go on in." I know that my friends and family are worried about me, but I have been avoiding them. It is not that I do not care about them or their well-being. It is sometimes easier to deal with things by myself.

When Harmony and Noelle walk into my room, a host of emotions of worry come flooding back. I do not know if it is because I missed them or if they remind me of the last time all four of us hung out at the spring dance. Tears stream down my face.

They both walk over to me giving me the tightest hug.

"It's okay, Drea," Harmony says, pushing my hair bonnet off my forehead. "We are here."

My sobs soon dissipate as all three of us sit there, hugging each other.

Noelle reaches for the tissue box on my nightstand. "We had to come and check on you. We've missed you at school. And you haven't returned any of our calls or texts."

"I'm sorry. I didn't know what to say."

"We heard you passed out in front of the school. Girl, we were so scared." Harmony hugged me again as if she wanted to make sure I were real.

"I'm okay. I just didn't feel like talking to anyone."

Noelle sat at my desk. "We understand that, but we still were worried about you and needed to see you. When are you coming back to school?"

"Monday."

"You think you'll be ready?"

"I'm not sure, but I can't stay in here forever."

"The good thing is we only have a few weeks left before summer break."

"I'm glad you can find the silver lining in all of this, Noelle," I say, getting back in bed.

"Oh, I didn't mean it like that. I'm so sorry." "It's okay. I know you didn't."

Noelle, lookingembarrassed, stares at the floor. Harmony comes and sit on the edge of my bed. "Have you spoken to his family?"

"No. I don't know what to say."

"There was an announcement at school yesterday that the funeral is going to be next Saturday. But they will have a memorial at school the following Monday from two to three-thirty."

"Oh, really?"

"Yeah. Everyone is sad and shocked this happened."

"They weren't too sad when they were laughing and bullying

him. They are just as responsible for his death." "You know some people are stupid, Drea."

"Yeah, but their stupidity drove Daniel to kill himself."

"I don't think that's fair to place all the blame on the folks at school. We have all been a part of gossip, whether it was true or not."

"Well, whose fault is it? The person who recorded and sent out that damn video?"

"Maybe. And it could be the entire community for judging him."

A feeling of anger starts to resurface without warning, creeping up in me like a dark cloud blocking out the sun. I can feel the heat rising in my chest. It is a familiar sensation, one that I have battled with since my parents' divorce and now Daniel's death.

"Drea, are you good?" Noelle asks, walking over to me. "Yeah, I'm good. I think I'm tired and need to take a nap."

Looking at each Noelle, Harmony ignores my discrete request of asking them to leave. "We can all walk to school together on Monday."

"Yeah, that will be fun, like we use to do before cheer, boyfriends, and . . . " Noelle's voice trail off. A look of embarrassment flushes her face.

"And what, Noelle?" I ask.

"Oh nothing." She flashes a quick smile. "I'm only saying, we all had a lot of stuff going on in our personal lives, and I want us to get back to the three amigos."

"You mean before I started hanging out with Daniel?" "No, I didn't say that."

"It sounds like you are saying that. Why else would you say like it used to be?"

I can see Noelle getting flustered, which does not happen often. "That's not what I meant."

"Yeah, Drea, chill out. Noelle is only trying to express how much she misses you and how close we used to be."

"No, she's not." Harmony jerks her head back like my words were trying to slap her. "You two were always jealous of me and Daniel's relationship. Y'all even thought we were dating. Y'all just couldn't stand that nerdy Drea could make friends outside of y'all.

For all I know, one of y'all could've made that video and sent it out to the school."

Noelle scrunches her face in disbelief, and Harmony stands up from my bed. "Are you serious? You take that back right now."

"Why should I, Harmony? It's how I feel."

"You don't know what you're feeling. How could me and Noelle record that video of Daniel and Christopher when we were on the dance floor with you? Don't get caught up in blaming people, especially the people who have always had your back. Remember, you were the one keeping secrets from us. You knew Daniel was gay."

"Yeah, so? He told me not to tell anyone, and besides, it wasn't my news to share."

"Yeah, well, don't go blaming me and Noelle for what someone else did. We haven't done anything but be there for you and you keep pushing us away. We are not your enemy, Drea. We are your friends; I thought your best friends. Come on, Noelle. Let's go."

"Drea, don't push us away," Noelle says, walking behind Harmony.

I lie on my bed and turn toward my window, unable to look at either one of them. Harmony's words are strong and direct, cutting right through me. But as much as they hurt, I know they are true.

The weight of the truth hangs heavily in the air, creating an uncomfortable silence.

As they both walk out of my room without saying another word, I am left alone with my thoughts. I can't wrap my head around why I got so mad at them and accused them of making the video. I know they would never do something so malicious. I guess I just need someone to blame. But now there is a larger hole in our friendship, and I do not know to fix it. I do not know how to fix myself. Why can't my life ever make sense?

CHAPTER ELEVEN

NOVEMBER 2022

Oliver decided not to stay and wait for his mother to pick him up. I probably freaked him out when I burst into tears after he asked me to be his girlfriend. Once we reached my house, I quickly said my goodbyes and went into the house. I knew he probably wanted more like another kiss or an answer to his question. But I could not offer him either.

"You're home already?" Mama asked while sitting at the kitchen table with Auntie Jolie. They look like they just finished an important conversation. "Is everything okay, honey?"

"Yes. I'm just tired," I said, walking past the kitchen and straight to my room. I crack my door so I can hear if they would talk about me or try to figure out what happened at the dance. I still cannot believe what Daniel told me.

"I wonder what got into her?" Mama asked Auntie Jolie. "I'm not sure, but I'll go back there in a minute."

"Ah, the fun teenage years," Mama said, slightly chuckling. "Remember Franklin when he was going through his teenage phase?

It was hell."

"So much you sent him to live in Chicago?"

Mama does not respond immediately. "That's not fair, Jolie, and you know it. Every boy needs to have a male figure in their life. Besides, he was getting out of hand with his behavior and grades. It just made sense that Franklin would go with his dad after the divorce."

"Look, all I know is Franklin had his problems, but Drea and Franklin were both happier when the family was all together. And so were you."

"Yeah, well, that's all water under the bridge now. I can't change the past."

Thick silence filled the kitchen. I don't hear any voices talking anymore. Until suddenly, I heard Mama say, "I'm going to lay down. Besides, I have to be back at work tomorrow."

"Are you good?"

"Yeah, I just need to be alone right now." "Okay, sis. I'll check on Drea."

I sat on the edge of my bed, staring at the walls of my room. I felt a familiar heaviness settle in my chest. It was a feeling I could not quite explain, but one that had become all too familiar in recent days. A mixture of sadness, frustration, and longing all rolled into one big ball of emotions. I tried to push it down, to ignore it and get ready for bed, but as always, it bubbled up and refused to be contained. I took in a deep breath, hoping to calm my racing heart, but it did little to ease the tightness in my chest. I closed my eyes, trying to focus on something else, anything else, but my mind kept going back to the source of my pain. Memories from tonight flooded my mind, each one more painful than the last. And then, without warning, tears began to flow down my cheeks again. I tried to wipe them away, but they came faster and harder than I could keep up with. I could feel a lump forming in my throat, making it difficult to breathe. No matter how hard I tried, I could not stop the cascade of emotions that threatened to overwhelm me. A sense of hopelessness washed over me as I realized that I was losing the fight against my emotions.

Gently knocking on my door, Auntie Jolie spoke in a whisper. "Drea, I know something is wrong. Can I come in, honey?"

I was trying to catch my breath, but it was getting harder. "I'm coming in, Drea." Auntie Jolie didn't wait for my response and slowly pushed my door open and saw me on the bed crying. I could feel her gentle arms wrap around me as she held me close to her chest, rocking me back and forth, assuring me that everything would be okay. "Calm down, Drea. Shh. Don't cry."

"He's, he's, he's gay." That was all I could get out before another round of tears streamed down my face.

"Shh, baby, it's okay. Calm down now."

Several moments went by before I was able to form words.

"Now tell me what happened, Drea."

I took in the deepest breath I could and slowly released it before trying to swallow the huge lump in my throat. "I saw Daniel at the dance. And he wanted to talk in the hallway. He apologized for how he treated me since last Saturday. I thought he was apologizing to ask me out because he really liked me. I really liked him. But he told me he was gay. None of this makes sense. Why would he be in Paisley's face and lead me on if he doesn't like girls?" I could feel the tears coming back as I buried my face into my aunt's chest.

"Come now, Drea. It's okay, baby." "No, it's not. Nothing is okay."

"Drea, listen to me." Auntie Jolie propped me up and looked me straight in the eyes. "Why are you really crying?"

"What do you mean? Daniel led me on this whole time." "Did he?"

"Yes, he did." I could feel anger creep in from her question. "Because sometimes we like to believe what we want to believe so we don't be uncomfortable."

"You don't think Daniel liked me like that?"

"I believe Daniel likes and value you as a friend and you wanted more. But to me his honesty is more commendable." "Commendable? Whose side are you on?"

"The side of truth. Drea, I know it hurts but remove your feelings for a moment. Daniel shared something so personal and sacred with you not because he 'likes' you but because he trusts you. And that's more powerful than anything."

"So I should be grateful he dumped that weight on me?"

"No, but just understand that you're not the only one hurting. That's all."

"Yeah, well, I can't feel that right now."

"Just give it time. One thing about time is that it's always there, you just have to use it wisely."

"Yeah."

"Get ready for bed and sleep off tonight."

With a gentle kiss to the forehead, Auntie Jolie walked out my room, closing the door behind her. After that conversation, I was filled with more confusion and anger. How did everything get so messed up? Why did it all come crashing down in an instant? The weight that Daniel dropped on me was a heavy burden that crushed my heart and soul. I feel lost, empty, and alone. There was so much to think about, but I finally took Auntie Jolie's advice and went to sleep.

The sun was shining through my window, casting a warm glow on my face, but I could not bring myself to fully embrace it. I slowly blinked away the grogginess and wiped away the eye crust. But I still could not shake off the bitter taste in my mouth. It was Sunday morning, the supposed day of rest and relaxation, but all I could feel was a lingering resentment in the pit of my stomach. I had known it was going to be a beautiful day when I saw the sun beaming through my window, but I could not bring myself to fully appreciate it. Instead, the weight of last night seemed to be pulling me back under the covers.

I lay there, reflecting on everything that happened and realized that I was still in a sour mood. My mind was clouded with negative thoughts, and my heart was heavy. I tried to push it aside and focus on getting ready for the day ahead, but it was a struggle. The usual excitement and anticipation for a lazy Sunday morning were nowhere to be found. Not wanting to face my family yet, I distracted myself by scrolling through social media. But seeing everyone else's seemingly perfect lives only added to my resentment. Funny videos and pictures from last night's dance filled my Instagram feed. It felt like everyone else had it all together while I was stuck in this never-ending rut of emotional confusion.

I scroll and stopped on a picture of Daniel and Paisley from last night. They looked like a real couple. So perfect. It was a lie. It made my stomach hurt more. But as I started to sink more into my spiral of harmful thoughts, a text came through. We need to talk.

Four words that sent a wave of uneasiness through my soul. It was from Daniel. I knew what he wanted to talk about, but I was not ready to face it. But at the same time, I could not ignore the message and pretend like everything was fine. I stared at my phone

for what felt like an eternity, trying to come up with a response. How could I possibly articulate the turmoil that was running through me with just a few words? I wanted to tell him that I was not ready to have this conversation. That I needed more time to process my feelings. That I feared what else he had to say. But instead, all I could come up with was:

When?

I saw the typing bubbles pop up immediately. Today. Like in an hour.

I look at the time on my phone: 10:31 a.m. Why did he want to meet so early on a Sunday?

He texted again: I can meet at your house.

Okay.

I slowly dragged myself out of bed and made my way into the bathroom, trying to avoid any interaction with my auntie. I wasn't ready to talk to her or anyone for that matter. I just needed some time to myself before facing this conversation with Daniel. As I stepped into the shower and allowed the hot water to cascade down my body, I felt a sense of relief washing over me. The warm water seemed to wash away some of my anxiety and stress, at least temporarily. I let the water relax my tense muscles and clear my mind, trying to prepare myself for the day ahead. But no matter how hard I tried, I could not shake off the feeling of unease.

I was not mentally prepared for this. But after my shower, I quickly got dressed and made my way to the kitchen, hoping to grab a cereal bar or something quick and escape back to my room without being caught. But that pursuit failed. My auntie was sitting at the table, her eyes locked on me. I tried my best to avoid her gaze and focus on getting my cereal bar, but she was not going to let me get out that easily.

"Good morning," she said with her eyes following me to the pantry.

"Good morning." "How did you sleep?" "Okay."

"Your mom left for work this morning. She's not working a double today."

I did not feel the need to respond because I knew Mama was gone. I grabbed my cereal bar and headed back to my room, but Auntie Jolie said, "You know your reality is only a mirror of what's inside of you."

I stopped and turned back, facing her. "What does that mean?"

"If you're always sad, judgmental, angry, and bitter on the inside, your external world is going to produce that. You attract what you are."

"So I attracted to be made a fool of by Daniel?"

"No. That's one of your life's lessons. How you're responding now, acting like the victim in this situation, will only produce more confusion and frustration."

My phone vibrated in my back pocket. Thinking it was Daniel, I grabbed it. The text read:

Hey. How are you? Can I see you today?

It was from Oliver. With a deep inhale and exhale, I tried to process what my auntie just said, the conversation I was about to have with Daniel, and now Oliver's texts. But there was no time left, the doorbell rung, and I knew it was him. I did not even have time to text Oliver back.

Chapter Twelve

It was not until I stepped outside and felt the warmth of the sun on my skin that something shifted inside me. It was like a tiny ray of hope breaking through the dark cloud. I took a deep breath and reminded myself that I could not let last night ruin my entire day.

But stepping onto the porch, I could not quite believe my eyes. Daniel was dressed in a gray and black tracksuit. He looked different. He looked like a normal boy. Grief was etched on his face, lines that were not there before were pronounced. The easy smile that used to light up his features was nowhere to be found. Instead, his gaze was distant and filled with sadness. It was a big contrast to the boy I used to know.

"Hey," I said, pulling the door behind me so Auntie Jolie would not hear our conversation.

"Hey. You want to walk around the neighborhood and just talk?"

"Sure."

The atmosphere was tense as we walked down the block.

Neither one of us spoke. Looking at my shoes provided the perfect distraction from not talking.

"Drea, I know I told you something very personal last night, and you left me standing there alone. I never thought you could do something like that." His voice sounded shaky and almost nervous. His tone was somber, one that matched his muted gray and black outfit. "I've never shared that secret with anyone, and I thought I could trust you."

"I don't know what you want me to say."

"I guess nothing. But I would appreciate it if you didn't tell anyone." Daniel's voice was sterner now.

"No, what I meant to say is I don't know what you want me to say about you feeling hurt I left you standing alone last night." I came to a stop, and I tried to gather the right words to express what I felt. "Daniel, I have liked you since the first day of school. And we got closer from working on our project. I really thought we would be good together, like in that way." I bit my bottom lip, pushing past my fear. "And when you stopped talking to me after I saw you playing in my closet, I didn't know why. Then for you to tell me last night you are gay was all too much."

"I never meant to lead you on. I really connect to you because you're a good person."

"Well, you looked very connected with Paisley too." "Oh, will you stop with the Paisley thing? I don't like that girl."

"Your actions speak differently."

"What do you mean? She asked me to the dance, not the other way around."

"And you said yes."

"And you went with that nerdy kid, Alton. Besides, I only played in your closet because you were in the bathroom so long shitting."

Ignoring my embarrassing moment he brought up, I said, "Oliver. His name is Oliver, and he treats me like the princess that I am. I even had my first kiss with him last night."

"Good for you."

"You know what? You asked to talk to me and now you're making me the bad guy? I don't even believe you're gay. I bet you're just saying that because you don't like me like that."

Daniel jerked his head back like he just smelled a stinky odor. "Excuse me? Are you serious? I just told you how you made me feel and I shared something very personal about myself, and you think I'm making it up so I don't have to go out with you? Get over yourself, Drea, because you're quite delusional."

At first, I was taken aback, as I am not someone who is easily angered. I am usually quiet and do not share how I really feel. But this time was different. It felt like something inside of me had awoken, a dormant volcano that suddenly erupted.

"First of all, you have been playing me and Paisley like instruments, leading us both on. If you never liked girls, you should've said that from the beginning."

"And you think this town would have accepted that?"

"Shut up! I'm talking." He shut his mouth quckly like I was throwing popcorn in it. "I don't know what everybody would've said, but I know what I would've said, but you didn't give me the chance. You just stopped talking to me, remember? From now on, we will only talk and work together to finish this project. Nothing else."

As I turned away, my heart was pounding with a mix of revenge and sadness. I could feel tears threatening to spill over,

but I refused to let him see me cry. I took a deep breath and tried to steady myself, but the emotional weight was overwhelming. In that moment, I felt like my entire world was crashing down around me. How did we get here? The thought alone was enough to bring tears to my eyes. But I refused to let him see my pain. I didn't want him to have that power over me. I started to walk away, trying to keep my composure. But my hands were shaking, and my breathing was uneven. I fought back the tears as I walked, not wanting him to see my vulnerability.

Walking back down the familiar path toward my house, I felt the colorful leaves crunching beneath my feet. It offered a soothing soundtrack to my thoughts. I let my mind wander to what just happened. I felt a sense of vindication and hope that my words had finally been heard. For months, I had been bottling up my feelings toward Daniel. But today, I could not take it anymore. I had reached my breaking point and decided to confront him about his behavior.

By the time I got back to my house, I saw that I had missed a call from both Oliver and Harmony. Instantly, a wave of guilt washed over me. I never responded back to Oliver, and I had not been keeping my besties in the loop.

Walking inside the house, I searched for the besties group chat in my phone and started to text.

"Drea are you okay?" Auntie Jolie asked from the kitchen. There was nowhere to retreat as I stood in the middle of the living room while I tried to text my real friends back.

"Yeah. I'm good."

"So that must have been Daniel? Very handsome." "His actions don't match his looks."

"You want to talk about it?"

"Nah, not really. I got everything off my chest when we talked."

"Oh you did, huh?"

"For the most part I did." I put my phone on the coffee table to focus on recounting our conversation. "He told me that he was hurt because I wasn't there for him when he told me his little secret. Like I asked for that." I sucked my teeth, feeling angry all over again.

"Hmm."

"I didn't yell, but I wanted him to understand how he made me feel. I don't want to be friends with a person like that. I walked away feeling like a weight had been lifted off my shoulders."

"You know I can hear it in your voice."

"What?"

"Hurt."

"Hurt? No, I feel good because I finally was able to speak my mind to him."

"Communicating effectively while listening to understand the other person's point of view and responding accordingly is speaking your mind. Your response was from the residue of hurt you haven't fully processed from last night."

"So you're on Daniel's side yet again?" "No, baby, I'm not."

"It sure feels like it."

"Let me ask you a question."

I released a deep sigh as I knew this might take a while, and I wanted to ride the wave of justification a little bit longer before I texted my friends and told them the scoop.

"How did you feel when your parents divorced?"

"What?" Why was she bringing this up again? "I don't know. Confused and angry."

"Why?"

"Auntie I really don't want to do this right now."

"Answer the question. Why did you feel confused and angry?"

"Because I didn't understand. Is that what you want to hear? I didn't understand why Mama and Daddy were breaking up. We were all so happy, and one day Daddy and Franklin were leaving."

"I know that hurts, baby. Your parents had problems, you just could not see it. Would you have been less angry and confused if they had talked to you beforehand? I don't know. However, Daniel has problems you couldn't see, but when he finally was able to talk to you, you shut him out." She came over and stood in front of me. "These are some confusing times in your life right now, but we all make mistakes. The grace you wanted during your parents' divorce is the same grace Daniel is asking for now."

I was not prepared to hear what she said. Her words seemed to come out of nowhere, and they hit me with such force that it took me a moment to register what she had just said. In that moment, my mind went completely blank, and my throat felt constricted. Her words were not meant to cause pain nor were they said with any malice. But they were raw and honest, and they forced me to

confront some uncomfortable truths about myself.

"So what should I do?" The way I told Daniel off felt good in the moment, but after hearing my auntie, I felt like shit.

"Only you can answer that but this time lead with this." She placed her hand on my heart and continued, "And not with this." She pointed to my head.

I spent the whole morning blaming Daniel, and only now did I realize that I was not so innocent either. Different scenarios danced around my head until it was interrupted by a notification. If a apologize to Daniel, would he forgive me? Could he forgive me?

Another text from Oliver.

Chapter Thirteen

As my alarm went off, I realized that I had barely slept. My mind kept racing. I tossed and turned all night, thinking about the dance, my conversation yesterday, and Daniel. What would I say to him today? He probably hated me for the way I treated him yesterday. But there was no time to think too much about it because I was meeting the girls in thirty minutes to catch them up on my life's gossip as we walked to school.

How could I have been so thoughtless? Why did I say those hurtful words to him? Guilt and regret were consuming me, and I knew that I had to face him today. But before I could dwell on it any longer, my phone vibrated.

See y'all in thirty!

Harmony had probably been up since five this morning.

Since she had Matthew, she has been acting more and more like an adult, including waking up at the crack of dawn.

As much as I wanted to stay in bed and avoid facing the world, I knew I could not back out on my friends. So I dragged myself out of bed and got ready for the day. Of course, Mama was not home, but Auntie Jolie was gone too. She did not leave a note, so I knew she had not gone back to Louisiana just yet.

Walking to our meeting spot, my mind kept replaying the events from yesterday. The way I had treated Daniel was unacceptable, and I knew I had to make it right, but I did not know how. The thought of seeing him made me nervous.

"Well, well, well, look who decided to show up to walk with us, Noelle?" Harmony yelled down the street when she saw me walking up.

"Girl, where have you been? I only seen you once at the dance." Noelle yelled out.

"And I heard you were looking fly as hell," Harmony added. "Oh, Harmony, you should've seen her. I ain't never seen our

girl look that good." They both started laughing. I giggled too so they would not suspect that the dance was the last thing on my mind. I had to put on a brave face and join in on their conversation. But as we started walking toward school, the anxiety and guilt started creeping back in. I needed to talk to them about what happened and get their advice. As we settled into a comfortable pace, I finally responded.

"Aunt Jolie got me all the way together. She made me look good."

"What did Oliver say when he saw you? Because he was eyeing you every time I saw him. And then y'all was gone. What happened?"

"Yeah, what happened? You know I have to live vicariously through you and Noelle."

"Oliver and I stepped into the side hallway and we . . . " My voice trails off as I see Oliver standing in front of the school as we walk up.

"Y'all what?" Harmony asked, forcing all of us to stop walking.

"We kissed."

Harmony and Noelle screamed. The sound of their voices pierced through the air, echoing across the schoolyard and catching the attention of everyone who were standing outside the school. I could see their faces were filled with joy and their eyes sparkled with excitement. Harmony and Noelle were jumping up and down, hugging each other tightly.

"Will y'all stop? Y'all are so embarrassing."

"Drea, this is huge. Your first kiss. Now you're like us. You finally kissed a boy."

"We aren't completely like you, honey. We don't have no babies," Noelle said to Harmony.

"Shut up, Noelle. You knew what I meant."

"I'm just playing. Jesus, some people can't take a joke anymore."

"Okay, okay. Anyway, I'll see y'all after school," I said,

trying to escape the conversation.

"Oh, so you leaving us now? I see Oliver over there. You two together now?"

I jerked my head back. "Um, no. What kind of question is that, Harmony?"

"A good question because I want to know too."

"Oh, Noelle. Not you too." They were not going to let me off the hook that easily. "No, we are not together."

Their eyes indicated they did not believe me, but I did not have time to try and convince them. Besides, I wanted to talk to them about Daniel, but time had run out. Oliver was walking toward me, and I did not want him to get ambushed by Harmony and Noelle.

"See y'all later." I walked over to Oliver before he could reach me.

"Hey, Oliver," I said casually as we walked into the building. "Hey, Oliver? That's it? I was calling and texting you all day yesterday. Did I do something wrong?"

"No, you didn't. I am so sorry I didn't get a chance to call you back. I had a family emergency."

The lie oozed out of my mouth so effortlessly that it almost made me want to vomit. It was a small lie, almost minor in the grand scheme of things, but as it slipped through my lips and into the world, I could not help but feel a tinge of guilt. It carried a burden that I knew I would have to bear. Lying had never come easy to me. As a child, I had been taught the importance of honesty and integrity. But I had lost sight of that advice in this moment.

"Is everything okay?"

"Oh, yes, we are all good." I couldn't look him in the eyes so I looked away staring at my locker and used itr as a distraction.

"Did you get a chance to think about what I asked you?"

Oliver asked as he met my eyes.

I paused, unsure of what to say. "I did think about it, and now is not a good time. I have a lot of stuff going on in my life." Now that was the truth.

Oliver looked deflated. He was a person who wore his emotions on his sleeve, and you could almost guess what he was feeling at any given time. But despite his apparent sadness, he still managed to put on a good front.

"I understand. Let me know if I can help with anything."

"Thank you so much for understanding Oliver." "Yeah. I got to get to class. I'll see you around."

Again, I felt like crap. Oliver was a great guy and would make a great boyfriend. But I just didn't have the time or energy to dedicate myself to a romantic relationship. I needed to focus on repairing the potential friendship I might have destroyed yesterday.

Walking into homeroom was nerve-racking. The sleek desk chairs, muted walls, and overwhelming smell of Mrs. Holmer's perfume seemed to taunt me as I took my seat in the back of the room. My heart raced as I realized that I would have to face Daniel. What would I say to him? How would I explain my sudden disappearance from his life? Would I apologize?

Daniel walked in just before the last bell rang. Heading to the empty seat next to me, he looked up and our eyes met. His expression was a mixture of anxiousness and sadness. I could tell that he was still hurt by my words.

"Hey," I said. I bit my bottom lip, feeling uneasy.

"Hey." He sounded cold and empty. He was still mad at me. I wanted to say more, but what?

"Alright, class. Everyone take your seat. I want to take attendance and go over the winter break packet you all are to complete over the break."

As Daniel settled into his seat, I looked over to see Paisley giving me the evil eye.

'What the hell is her problem?' I asked under my breath.

As Mrs. Holmer discussed extra credit work over the winter break, I could not concentrate. All I could think about was how I was going to approach Daniel now. In my mind, I ran through different scenarios: apologizing, explaining myself, and asking for forgiveness, but none of them seemed good enough. When the bell finally rang, I took a deep breath and turned to Daniel. His eyes met mine once again.

I finally spoke up. "I'm sorry," I said, my voice trembling. "I'm sorry for my ugly, inconsiderate words. I am sorry for hurting you."

After a brief silence, he said, "I forgive you, and I'm sorry too, Drea. I didn't realize I was leading you or Paisley on."

"Wait, but you have to know Paisley likes you."

"Yeah, I know she likes me, but I didn't think I was leading her on."

"In her mind, you and her were a thing. That's why she's probably giving me the evil eye today."

Daniel made a weird face. I got the feeling he might know something he didn't want to tell me.

"I don't think that's the reason she's giving you the evil eye."

"How do you know?"

"After you left me at the dance, I went back into the gym and told Paisley I had to leave too. When she asked why, I told her you and I had a disagreement, and I needed to follow you home to talk."

"What? Are you freaking serious? Why would you tell her that? Now she thinks I stole her man." I rub my temples.

"It's not like I lied. We did have a disagreement, and I did follow you home, but I left after I saw Oliver walking you up to your porch."

"You followed me home?"

"Yeah. I didn't like how the conversation ended, and you walked off so quickly I couldn't tell you I was sorry for making you feel that way."

"I don't know what to say." My shoulders slumped.

"I'm not trying to make you feel guilty. I'm just letting you know why Paisley is probably giving you the evil eye." "I guess that's what I get for not talking to you."

"We are all still learning. By the way." His voice got very low, making it almost impossible to hear him. "Did you tell anyone about what I told you?"

"No. Of course not. I was pissed at you, but I didn't tell anyone."

"I would appreciate it if you didn't." "I know, and I wont."

The bell rang again.

"You ready to go to our next class?" I asked with a huge smile glued on my face. Daniel smiled back.

"Yeah, let's get out of here."

And just like that, I got my friend back.

CHAPTER FOURTEEN

It was an art navigating high school hallways. You had to be able to maneuver through the crowd without getting trampled or lost. That is why Daniel was holding my hand so we could bypass the traffic to get down the hallway to our next class. Yet Oliver did not understand that. So, when I bumped into him, he nearly burst a blood vessel. His eyes got large, and he could have killed Daniel with them.

"I was about to say excuse me until I realized it was you."

I let go of Daniel's hand as he looked back. The crowd of students carried him to our next class.

"I'll catch up with you," I yelled at Daniel.

"So, are you and Daniel a thing? Is that the real reason you don't want to be my girlfriend?"

"Of course not."

"Of course not, what?"

The bell rung again. One more bell, and I'd be considered late.

"Daniel and I are not a thing, and that is not the reason I can't be your girlfriend."

"Why you can't be my girlfriend? We kissed each other.

Didn't that mean anything?"

"Oliver, I told you I have a lot going on in my life right now."

"Does some of that has to do with Daniel?" "Oh my God, Oliver, no. I gotta go."

After getting into Mr. Fitzgerald's class, I made my way to our shared table. Daniel's eyes followed me.

"What happened to you? One minute you were behind me, and next minute, you weren't."

"I ran into Oliver, and he thought there was something going on."

I said with a sly giggle, "If only he knew."

"Hey, you want to come over to my house after school? My mom bought a new battery for our project, and I really think it's going to work this time."

"Sure. I'll text my mama and auntie and let them know."

Autumn Crest was a cute and bougie neighborhood located just a fifteen-minute walk from our school. This area was like my other home. Noelle lives in this neighborhood, but I was always amazed how perfect this neighborhood was. Daniel and I walked through the streets. I noticed and remembered how different this area was from my busy neighborhood.

Our destination was Daniel's house, which was tucked away in the heart of Autumn Crest, several blocks from Noelle's house. As we made our way toward his house, I took in the sights and peaceful sounds of this neighborhood. The streets were lined with trees, although their leaves had disappeared. It was the only sign that fall had arrived. The air was fresh and warm, a welcome change from the stuffy hallways of our school. Each of the houses was unique, exuding a sense of warmth and coziness. It was evident that the people living in this area took great pride in maintaining their homes.

We laughed and joked as if we had known each other for years and nothing happened just the weekend before. And at that moment, I knew that Daniel was going to be a lifelong friend.

"I hope you have tough skin," Daniel said after his last joke about our principal Mrs. Braun.

"That was random. Why do you say that?"

"My parents, more like my father, can be a little difficult." "Oh, I don't care about that. Besides, we are just friends." Daniel stopped walking. He looked nervous.

"What's wrong?" I asked, searching his eyes for a clue. "My parents don't know."

"What? That you're gay?"

"Yes. They wouldn't understand so please don't say anything."

"I promised you I wouldn't tell anyone."

Letting out a deep sigh, he said, "Thanks, Drea."

We soon arrived at Daniel's house, a beautiful two-story home with a neatly manicured lawn. I stepped into his house and felt a sense of awe wash over me. The pristine white carpet and walls gave the space a sense of elegance and sophistication, almost like a museum. Unsure of what to do, I stood frozen by the door, wondering if I should take off my shoes or simply admire the decor from the front door. It was not just the whiteness of the interior that caught my attention, but the way everything seemed to blend seamlessly together. There were no bold colors or eye-catching patterns to distract from the overall aesthetic of the space. Instead, everything was carefully selected and placed, creating a sense of harmony throughout.

I took off my shoes and cautiously made my way into the living room. I felt a bit self-conscious.

"I see why you said what you said., I whispered to Daniel, but he pretended not to hear me as he walked in front of me.

My shoes, now in hand, seemed to stand out against the pure whiteness of the carpet. I was afraid to make a misstep or do anything that might disrupt the perfect balance that had been created. Following Daniel, I made my way further into the house. I admired the attention to detail in every aspect of the decor. Even the furniture seemed carefully chosen to complement the white theme. The couches, chairs, and tables were all sleek and modern, adding to the overall sense of sophistication.

I sat down on the sofa, trying my best not to disturb its pristine appearance. I wondered about the upkeep and maintenance required to keep this house looking like a museum. Every inch of this house exuded a sense of elegance and finesse that was hard to find in most homes.

"I'll be right back," Daniel said, walking through a pair of French doors that probably led to another immaculate part of the house.

While sitting there, a thought came to me. The color white often symbolized purity and perfection. And in this house, it was evident that this was true. I felt a newfound appreciation for the color and the sense of calm and tranquility it brought to this space.

"Well, hello there," a beautiful woman said, walking next to Daniel.
"I'm Mrs. Gardner"

His mother was stunning. Her hourglass, shape was simply captivating. Her features were stunning. Her complexion was unlike any other, a rich honey color that glowed against the white room. It was hard to believe that she was just a regular woman living in Coral Bluff.

"Hello, Mrs. Gardner. I'm Andrea Ramsey." My mouth seemed to go dry as I remembered my name.

"It's a pleasure to meet you. Would you like something to drink? Water? Tea? Lemonade?"

"Water, please."

Daniel motioned me to follow them.

"Oh, you don't have to carry your shoes. You can leave them by the door," she said as she elegantly walked away.

After placing my shoes by the door, I hurried behind them, making sure not to touch anything.

"Danny Bear doesn't have many friends to come over since we moved here." She opened a glass bottle of San Pellegrino sparkling water. "Where are you from?"

Giggling to myself from Daniel's nickname, I responded, "Here. I stay about fifteen minutes away." "Oh, wow. That's close."

"That's the house I've been going over to work on my science project. She's my partner." Daniel said, opening himself a bottle of water.

"Oh, I see. And that Paisley girl?"

I take a sip of my water. I was pleasantly surprised by its taste. I had never had water out of a glass bottle and certainly not sparkling water. The bubbly texture and crisp flavor tickled my throat, but it was so refreshing.

"We are just friends, Mother."

"Okay, there's no need to get defensive. Anyway, do you have any siblings?" She directs her attention back to me.

"Yes, ma'am. I have an older brother." "He goes to the same high school?" "Mom, why are you interrogating her?"

"I just want to know a little bit about the friends you're hanging around. Is that a crime?"

"No, ma'am. He doesn't go to our school. He lives in Chicago with our dad." As soon as the words left my mouth, I felt a pinch of guilt in the pit of my stomach, and a sense of shame washed over me. Embarrassed my home life was broken and the total opposite of Daniel's perfect home, I wanted to hide under the table.

"Chicago, huh?" Mrs. Gardner asked, leaning over the black- and-white granite kitchen island. "I love that city. Have you been to Chicago?"

"Yes, ma'am. I go during winter, spring, and summer break." I took a sip of my refreshing sparkling water and heard the front door open.

"That must be your father, Daniel," she said as she sprang into action. She made her way to the stove and immediately picked up the tea kettle and filled it with water. After placing it on the stove for it to boil over the high heat, within seconds, Mrs. Gardner performed the best rendition of making tea for her husband. It seemed like everything she did was intentional and flawless.

And right when I thought Daniel's family could not get any more perfect, his daddy walked into the kitchen.

"Hello, honey. Your tea will be ready soon."

He did not say anything. His eyes scanned the room before locking in on me. His eyes were a deep shade of brown that seemed to hold a world of secrets. They were curious yet guarded, a perfect reflection of his mysterious persona. It reminded me of my mother's eyes after Daddy left. I could sense that this was a man who had seen the world and experienced both its beauty and its darkness.

And it was evident in the lines that crinkled around his eyes and the slight stubble on his jawline.

"I see we have a guest."

"Oh, yes, honey. This is Andrea, Daniel's friend." "Friend, huh?"

"Yes, Dad, my friend." It was clear that Daniel's mood had shifted as he sat in the kitchen next to me. Moments before, we were outside, laughing and joking. Now, he appeared annoyed; his brows were crumpled, and his body language was closed off. This change in demeanor was noticeable, but his dad did not acknowledge it.

"I'm Mr. Gardner. It's a pleasure to have you in our home." "Thank you, Mr. Gardner." He was so formal, but he matched the house. Daniel's parents both matched the picture-perfect home and neighborhood.

"We have to get going. We have to finish up our project," Daniel said just as the tea pot started to whistle.

"You're leaving already? I just got home."

"We were going to go back to Drea's house and work on the project there."

I glanced at Daniel, not saying a word. I remember he said we would work on the project at his house, but I guess he wasn't expecting his father to be home.

"So, you don't have room in this big ass house to work on your project here?" Mr. Gardner's question had a arrogance wrapped around it. "Nonsense. You can work on your project right here."

"Here's your tea." Mrs. Gardner gently placed the cup on the island next to Mr. Gardner's hand.

Daniel let out a sigh.

"Is there a problem?" Mr. Gardner remained standing, and the mood had definitely shifted.

"No, sir," Daniel said, looking down.

"Good. Besides, it's not every day that you bring a girl home." He turned to me and picked up his teacup. "It was a pleasure meeting you, and hopefully I'll see more of you with my son. I'll be in my office preparing for my closing arguments tomorrow, Camilla. I do not want to be disturbed."

"Of course, honey."

Daniel rolled his eyes and motioned to follow him. As I followed him up the stairs to his bedroom, I felt a sense of unease. The lavish decor and luxurious surroundings of Daniel's home continued to captivate me, but now, as I walked behind him, I could feel tension and coldness in the air. The house itself was out of a magazine, but as I made my way through the hallway leading to his room, I noticed the lack of warmth and love in this seemingly perfect home.

Making my way to Daniel's room, I expected to find a room filled with a little clutter. However, Daniel's bedroom was not a teenager's room or at least not my room. It was almost scary how orderly and neat his room was, with everything seemingly in its rightful place. I admired how clean his room was for a guy. The first thing that caught my eye was the bed. It was perfectly made, with crisp sheets and fluffed pillows. It was almost like walking into a hotel room rather than a teenager's bedroom. I wondered if Daniel made his bed like this every day or if it were just a one-time thing. My eyes searched the room, and I noticed that there were no clothes scattered on the floor or piled up on a chair. In fact, there were barely any clothes visible in the room at all. My brother should take some notes from Daniel.

"Damn, Daniel. I've never been in a more perfect room, not even my mama's."

He did not respond. He just sat at his desk and stared out the window like he was waiting for someone. Even the desk in his room was perfectly organized. There were no papers or books sprawled across the top, but instead, everything was neatly placed in its designated spot. Daniel had a calendar on the wall, which was color-coded with different tasks and events.

"Are you okay?"

"Yeah. I'm good."

"It doesn't seem like you're good. Your whole mood changed. What's up?"

"Nothing. Let's just work on this project so I can walk you home."

Chapter Fifteen

Present Day

Decisions, decisions. Sometimes life throws us a curveball that leaves us feeling unsure and confused. Right now, I am struggling with one of those curveballs as Dr. E's words continue to dance around in my head. How can I teach people about compassion when I cannot even control my own emotions? I am still unsure if I will attend Daniel's funeral, let alone his memorial service at school. Dr. E says I am getting stronger, but in this very moment, I feel like I can break at any time.

Now sitting in my room, thumbing through half-written sheets of paper, I try to complete Dr. E's original homework assignment. Writing a forgiveness letter to a person who is no longer here is more difficult than I thought. How do I sum up the impact he had on my life while telling him how much he hurt me by taking his life? How do I find the strength to say goodbye to someone who brought so much joy and inspiration into my life?

The vibration from my phone distracts me from my thoughts.

Instagram notifications. I do not know how I will be able to get anything done with so many distractions. Putting my head down, I take a deep breath in and slowly release the anxiety that was building up in my chest.

"Drea," Auntie Jolie says through my cracked door. "Yes, ma'am?"

Pushing my door open, she invites herself in my room. "Are you hungry?"

"No."

"Are you doing schoolwork?"

"No. I finished that earlier."

Turning around from my desk, I see Auntie Jolie sit on my bed. Her posture indicates that she had something to say.

"Your mom said you were quiet in the car on our way from your counseling session this morning. Is everything okay?"

"Yes. Well, I don't know."

"Tell me what's on your mind, honey."

"I'm not sure if I want to go to Daniel's funeral on Saturday." "Why wouldn't you go? Was he not one of your best friends?"

"I'm afraid I won't be able to keep it together and will break down in front of everyone. I've already had a panic attack at school.

That's embarrassing."

"No, it's not, honey. It shows that you really cared for him and his death deeply hurts you. His presence in your life meant a lot to you. It's your body's way of saying you're grieving.

"I think it's grief and anger." "What do you mean?"

"Dr. E said I have some resentment toward Daniel because he took his life. And now Dr. E wants me to write a forgiveness letter to Daniel while teaching people compassion for other people. I really don't understand."

"Writing the forgiveness letter to Daniel is not for him; it's for you."

"What do you mean?"

"You must release the hurt and disappointment you feel toward his decision to take his life. You may not understand why, but he felt like at that moment there was no other choice. You may not like it, but you must try to accept it. And once you can do that, you will know what compassion feels like, and you can show it to others."

Tears fill my eyes. I walk over to my auntie and collapse in her arms. The weight of guilt and despair is too much to accept, and I needed her comfort more than ever. In that moment, strong or not, I can not hold back my tears any longer. I bury my face in her shoulder, and I feel a sense of relief come over me. It is almost like her arms are a safe haven, shielding me from all the chaos and turmoil that is swirling inside of me. And as the tears continue to flow, I can feel myself slowly letting go of all the pent-up anger and resentment that I had been holding back.

"When will I stop grieving? When will my heart stop hurting?" I ask through my tears.

"Losing someone close to us is never easy, Drea. It shakes us to our core and changes us in ways we could never imagine. But instead of hiding our pain and trying to move on quickly, we should allow ourselves to grieve and heal at our own pace. It's not about how we grieve or how long it takes us to move on. It's about honoring the memories of what you and Daniel shared."

For the next several moments, I let her words penetrate me. My auntie does not say anything else. She holds me close and lets me cry. And that is all I need in this moment.

Will I ever fully heal and understand compassion? After losing my best friend, I do not believe it. How could time erase the pain and emptiness I feel? Since he left this world, each morning I wake up with a heavy heart and a cloud of sadness hanging over me. Until today.

Chapter Sixteen

December 2022

The few weeks left in the first semester seemed to fly by as we worked on our electric ropeway. When it came to presenting our project to the class, we knew each other's parts word for word.

Standing in front of the class, our confidence was contagious, engaging everyone in the room. Well, almost everyone. Paisley did not seem to be impressed.

Our electric ropeway was not only functional but visually appealing.

"Great job, partner," I said, giving him a soft shove as he placed our ropeway on the counter in the lab.

"I must say, you, my friend, are the smartest person I know.

Well, besides me."

We both laughed and made our way to lunch. Still relishing our achievements, we did not pay any attention to the other students in the crowded hallway until Harmony stopped us both in our tracks.

With her hands on her hips and with no smile in sight, she said, "So how long are you going to continue to ghost your best friends?"

Stopping mid-laugh, I realized I'd been spending most of time with Daniel.

"I mean you don't even walk with us anymore," Harmony continued. "Did you even know Noelle made captain of the cheer squad?"

"What? No."

"You see? You've been missing everything."

"I'll catch up with you at lunch," I said to Daniel.

"I'll save you a seat. Hi, Harmony. Bye, Harmony," Daniel said, too afraid to look at her, fearing her anger would spill over to him.

"Uh-uh," Harmony said, rolling her eyes. "I mean, you can at least text back on our group chat."

"I'm so sorry, Harmony. I've just been so caught up in this science project, I lost all concept of time."

"No, you mean you've been all caught up with your new boyfriend Daniel."

That was a clear misconception, but I couldn't tell Harmony the truth about Daniel.

"It's not like that, Harmony."

"Oh yeah? Then what is it like? I have a baby, and I still make time for my friends."

"You're right, and I'm sorry. I promise I'm going to be a better friend. Especially since our project is over."

"Hell, the semester is over."

"Let's do something before I leave for Chicago next weekend. Me, you, and Noelle."

"Like what?"

"Let's have a sleepover at my house this weekend like we used to. We can stay up all night, eat pizza until our stomachs hurt, and catch up on all the school's gossip. It'll be fun."

"You're trying to bribe me?"

"I'm trying to get my friend to stop being mad at me." "Uh-huh. Well, it's working."

"I'll text our group and let Noelle know."

"Okay. I'll see if Granny is down with keeping Matthew overnight."

"So we're good?"

"We're good. Just don't shut us out, Drea."

"Deal."

Friday slipped by like any other day, but somehow this Friday brought a sense of anticipation and excitement. Maybe it's because I got to spend time and catch up with my besties or maybe it was the fact that I knew I would be leaving next week for Chicago.

My excitement was expanded when I found out Mama and Auntie Jolie were going out. It was a rare occasion when Mama and Auntie decided to go out together. Most days, Mama was either at work or sleeping; her demanding job as a nurse left her exhausted. Auntie Jolie, on the other hand, rarely came to town and didn't stay longer than a couple of weeks. So when they both announced that they were going out, I knew it must be something special.

Seeing Mama take a break from her daily routine was a welcome change. As they got ready, I could see the excitement in their eyes. It was as if they were teenagers going out on a double date. They laughed and whispered, picking out their outfits and doing each other's hair. It was touching to see them bonding like this; something that I rarely got to witness. As they left the house, I could feel their excitement. I knew that this was their time, and they deserved it.

Now sitting in my room, listening to music and laughing with Noelle and Harmony, I was reminded of how we used to be when we were in middle school. We did not have a care in the world. We were no longer the naive middle schoolers we once were, but rather, we were strong and courageous teenagers carving our own paths in the world. But despite our differences and the challenges we faced individually, our friendship remained a constant source of support and happiness. There was a sense of comfort in knowing that no matter what happened, we always had each other's backs.

"Pass me the charger. I'm at twenty percent," Noelle said, plopping herself on the edge of my bed with a vacant expression. Looking at her, made it clear that something was wrong. Although, Noelle always stood out as a daydreamer. From the time we first met in second grade, I could recall multiple instances where her mind seemed to be elsewhere. Whether it was during class, lunch, or playground activities, she was constantly lost in thought.

"Girl, are you okay?" I asked Noelle, handing her my charger. I often wondered what was going on inside her head as she drifted off into her own world. As a child, I assumed she must have been bored or uninterested in our activities. But as we got older and remained friends, I came to understand that daydreaming was simply a part of who Noelle was.

"Uh, yeah. Why wouldn't I be okay?"

"Sometimes you get stuck in your head and aren't involved in the convo."

"Maybe y'all conversations don't interest me," Noelle said with a sly smile sliding across her beautiful face.

"Girl, shut up," Harmony chimed in, grabbing another slice of pepperoni pizza. "You're just as messy as me and Drea. Speaking of, what's the scoop on you and Daniel? You've been spending a lot of time with him."

"I told y'all we were working on our science project."

"So you mean to tell me that nothing went on between you and Danny boy?"

Harmony and Noelle laughed at Harmony's nickname Danny Boy. I didn't have the heart to tell them the nickname his mother called him.

"It's Daniel, and yes, nothing happened between us."

"Oh, someone is touchy," Noelle said as she halfway listened while she scrolled on her phone. "What about Oliver?"

"Yeah, Oliver has been low-key distant," Noelle added.

"Yes, Oliver and I shared a kiss."

"Your first kiss might I add," Harmony said.

Rolling my eyes, I said, "Yes my first kiss. But he wanted more, and I wasn't ready."

"Wait! He wanted to go all the way?" Noelle ears magically perked up then.

"Eww, no. Your mind is always in the gutter. He wanted to be my boyfriend."

"Oliver is a good guy, Drea. Why didn't you want to be his girl?"

"Yeah, it's not every day a guy is knocking on your door." "Shut up, Noelle! Everyone isn't entertaining multiple guys like you."

"Oh, please, Harmony. You're the one who got pregnant."

I instantly saw the hurt flush over Harmony's eyes. She carried the weight of her responsibility on her shoulders, trying to provide for her child and give him the best life possible. But instead of receiving encouragement and understanding from her best friend, she was met with disapproval and reminders about the consequences of her actions. Perhaps the most painful reminder of her situation was the fact that her own best friend, someone she thought would always be there to support her, judged her.

"That's not fair, Noelle, and you know it," I said.

"No, it's okay. She likes to take digs at me and bring up past mistakes. But it's okay. My son is the best thing that ever happened to me." I could see Harmony's eyes looking glassy, like she was fighting back the tears. "I've never judged you, Noelle. Not even when you talk about how much you can't stand your biological parents for giving you up for adoption."

"Okay, ladies. This was supposed to be a fun sleepover like we used to have. Now you two are taking mean and cheap shots at each other. Are we best friends or not?"

"Noelle started it."

"Harmony is right. Noelle, you did start it once again."

"I'm sorry, okay?"

"No, it's not okay. You always bring up that fact I got pregnant. Yes, I made a dumb mistake, but my son is no mistake."

Noelle placed her phone on the bed and did not respond

immediately. Harmony wiped away a tear that escaped her eye. Harmony had always been a strong-willed person who never wanted anyone to see her cry.

"I know your son is not a mistake. I admire you for not giving up your son like my parents gave me up."

Noelle's voice was sad, but steady. The room was quiet. The sky outside was dark. And the only sound that could be heard was the gentle rustling of leaves in the wind outside my window and Kehlani's Blue Water Road album on shuffle. I thought about what Harmony and Noelle said, and my heart went out to them both. It was not easy to open up and share your pain with others, even if they are your best friend. It takes a lot of courage to let someone see the raw and unfiltered version of yourself. And yet, they both were baring their soul to each other. In that moment, I realized the true depth of our friendship. We saw each other through many highs and lows, but this was different. It was a moment of complete vulnerability and honesty.

We sat in silence for a few minutes before Harmony finally spoke. "Noelle, I am sorry you carry that feeling, but you are amazing. And your parents love you. Hell, we love you too, even when you get on our damn nerves." We all giggled, wiping tears from our eyes. "But you don't have to feel like no one wants you. You're a bad bitch! Period."

"That's right. We all know Noelle has a bad-bitch complex!" I said, teasing her.

"Thank you both, and Harmony, I am really sorry for always taking digs at you."

"No worries. You're still my bestie."

"I love y'all."

"We love you too, Drea." Harmony and Noelle said as we all erupted with laughter.

Our laughter died down, and we scrolled through Instagram and Snapchat before we finally made our own pallets on the floor and bed. I felt a surge of love and appreciation for these amazing girls. We had seen each other at our best and our worst, and yet, we continue to love and support each other unconditionally. In a world where friendships were often underestimated and undervalued, I was grateful to have these incredible girls by my side. Drifting off to sleep, I could help but to look forward to the years to come and the memories we would create together. Because no matter how old we got, we would always be in each other's lives.

CHAPTER SEVENTEEN

There was something special about Chicago winters. A fleeting thought of what our family winter vacations used to look like popped in my mind as I looked out my window seat as we were about to land at Midway Airport. One of my favorite things about Chicago in the winter was the way the snow crunched under my Ugg boots as I walked down the streets. It was a sound that was so distinctly winter. It brought back memories of my childhood when we used to come up every Christmas and spend time with Grandma Bonnie, my dad's mother. Franklin and I would spend days playing in the snow for hours with both of us vowing to never be the first to throw the last snowball.

When I walked off the plane, reality hit me as the bite from the cold and still air slapped me on the back of my exposed neck. My pace picked up to a brisk walk as I made my way through the jet bridge to baggage claim. And then I saw him.

"Daddy!" I yelled, skipping two steps off the escalator. I ran to him as he was standing by baggage claim number three. My daddy was one of the handsomest men I knew. His smooth, dark skin radiated love, and his bright, optimistic energy was contagious. His appearance might be casual with a pair of jeans and a flannel shirt under his bubble coat, but there was an unmistakable elegance that came from him.

"Drea! Let me take a look at you. Oh, wow! You've grown a whole foot and keep getting prettier. You're going to give Beyonce a run for her money."

"Aww, Daddy, you know I haven't grown that much."

I buried my head in his stomach. His tall, strong body always put me at ease; I knew I would always be safe with him. "Let's get your bag and head home."

"Is everyone there?" "Franklin is at work. And—" "Work? Franky has a job?"

"Yeah, he has a job. Why wouldn't he?"

"I don't know. You didn't tell me he had a job when we talked."

"Yeah, well, he'll be home later tonight. But your grandmother prepared your favorite."

"Smothered chicken and potatoes?"

"Yep."

As soon as I stepped out of the airport and into the crisp air, I could feel a certain energy that only this city could provide. The streets might be covered in snow and the wind might be biting, but to me, it was all part of the magic.

"I'm so glad to be back."

"Me too, honey. Two weeks isn't long enough." "When are you coming back to Coral Bluff?"

"Coral Bluff?" He looked confused. "Why on earth would I go back there? My life is here in Chicago, honey." "Yeah, I guess." Walking to the car, I turned my attention to the city so I did not think about Daddy and Franklin being hundreds of miles away from me and Mama.

While daddy drove, I sat in the passenger seat like a tourist. I noticed the hustle and bustle of people going about their day. Despite the cold weather, there was an undeniable buzz in the air. Locals and tourists alike were bundled up in their warmest coats, scarves, and hats, eagerly making their way to their destinations. The holiday spirit was in full force, with festive lights adorning buildings and holiday music playing in shops and restaurants. But it was not just the holiday spirit that made Chicago in the winter so special. There was a certain beauty to the city in its winter coat. The snow blanketed everything, creating a serene and peaceful atmosphere. The buildings seemed to sparkle in the sunlight, and the city skyline was even more breathtaking with a snowy backdrop.

"Alright, honey, we are home. I'll put your suitcase in your room."

"Thanks, Daddy."

Walking into Grandma's house, the smell of a homecooked meal greeted me. It was a familiar smell that immediately put me at ease and reminded me of what Coral Bluff used to be. Now I had become familiar with leftovers made while I was at school or takeout.

"Grandma Bonnie."

"Andrea! Lord have mercy! Come here, child." Her bear hug nearly crushed my spine, but her breast and stomach comforted me like a body pillow. "I made your favorite."

"Yes, ma'am. Daddy told me."

"Stand back and let me get a good look at you."

I paraded around like I was competing for Miss America.

"Look at you. Just as pretty as the day you were born, looking like your daddy."

We both giggled, and she scooped me back into her arms for another extended hug.

"Alright, Mama. Let Drea get settled in so she can eat." "I'm sorry, baby. I'm just so glad you're back."

"Me too, Grandma."

I walked toward the guest room that served as my room when I was in town. I tossed my book bag on the bed and lay across the bed while reaching for my phone. I sent a quick text to Mama and the girls that I made it took every bit of five seconds. I checked Instagram and then Snapchat. My mind traveled to Daniel and wondered what he may be doing. I sent him a text.

What's up? I made it to Chicago.

'Good.

What you doing?

Hating my life as I do last minute Christmas shopping with my mother.

LOL! But you love shopping Correction: I love shopping for me. Bribe her into getting you something. She won't take the bait.

I send the crying and laughing emoji. So you're going to tell them?

I don't know why I texted that. We were having a lighthearted conversation, and I just made it turn serious. I waited for the bubbles to pop up, but it did not.

"Come on, baby. Your food is going to get cold." Grandma voice, full of excitement, came from the kitchen.

"Coming." Putting down my phone, I tried not to think about what Daniel might be thinking from my last text. Instead, I would rather enjoy my family and the holidays.

A plate made for a queen met me at the table. Grandma and Daddy were already sitting down.

I complimented the chef again and said, "This looks good, Grandma."

"Thank you, baby. Let me bless this food. Dear Heavenly Father, thank you for allowing our baby girl to travel safely to us. Bless her comings and goings as well as Franklin, Shane, and myself. Father, even bless Bianca. We thank you for this food we
are about to receive. Amen."

"Nice prayer, Mama," Daddy said with a smirk on his flawless face.

"So how are you doing in school?" "I'm doing well, Grandma."

"Yeah, Mama. Drea is in all honor classes this year, and she's killing it. Aren't you, honey?"

"Yeah, Daddy, I'm killing it." I giggle as I fight with a piece of chicken that refuses to stay in my mouth.

"Oh, I know my granddaughter is smart. Andrea, did you know Shane took advance classes when he was your age and graduated high school at sixteen?"

"You did, Daddy?"

If embarrassment were a person, it would have been my daddy. He was very modest when it came to talking about himself and his accolades. "Aww, Mama, come on now. I'm sure Drea isn't interested in my high school years."

"Oh, yes, I am. Tell me more, Grandma. How was Daddy with girls?"

"Alright now."

"You hush it, Shane. Your daddy has always been respectful yet shy around girls."

"No, I was not, Mama."

"Quit lying. You had the biggest crush on . . . What was that light-skin gal's name from over East? Maria. Maggie."

"Meagan," he says reluctantly.

"That's it. Meagan. He loved him some Meagan, but she would not give him the time of day."

More interested, I leaned forward and asked, "Why not?" "Who knows? Maybe my Shane was too straight and narrow for her. She was fast anyway. Whatever happened to her?" "I have no idea, Mama."

"How did you and Mama meet, Daddy?"

"Oh, now he was in love with your mama. He told me he knew he was going to marry Bianca the first time he saw her at Tuskegee."

"Alright, that's enough. Don't start filling her head up with nonsense, Mama."

"What nonsense? I'm speaking the truth."

Ignoring Grandma, Daddy said, "Finish up and get ready for bed. I have a full day planned with you tomorrow."

"What are we doing, Daddy?"

"It's a surprise, but it does involve Navy Pier."

Grandma rolled her eyes as she knew her gossiping must wait for another day.

"OMG, I love Navy Pier. Is Franky coming too?" "Yep. It's going to be like the old days when we used to come up here for the holidays."

"Except your wife isn't here," Grandmas shadily said under her breath.

"That's enough, Mama."

I sat there confused about why Daddy got so irritated at Grandma for sharing family stories. He had always loved talking about the family and goofy stuff. I wondered what was going on with Daddy. But I dared not ask. I did not know if he would tell me if I would ask.

"I'm about to take my shower. I'm tired from traveling." I needed to break the awkwardness of our dinner.

"Put your plate in the sink."

"Thank you, Grandma, for that dinner. It hit the spot."

"You're welcome, baby."

After what felt like a spa shower with the multiple shower heads peeping from overhead and my sides, I stood in front of the mirror. I thought about my grandma's words. Why won't Daddy or Mama talk to me about their life? About their divorce? About each other? It was a question that had been lingering in my mind for quite some time. I wanted to understand why my parents could not make it work, why they chose to separate. I wanted to know their side of the story.

But those thoughts and questions had to be answered another day because I was tired and sleepy. I put on my favorite oversized pajama set, and I snuggled up under my Downy-smelling sheets. I was excited to be with my dad, have a fresh home cooked meal, and get some much-needed sleep.

I planned on sleeping until my body naturally woke up. So cutting off the Monday through Friday alarm was a must. And then I saw Daniel's text: I will tell them on Christmas Day.

CHAPTER EIGHTEEN

Daniel was not a common face at Oak Valley High. His tall and solid frame was an impressive figure among his peers. The boys in his grade lacked maturity and refinement. They loved their baggy jeans and slick remarks that always had a sexual undertone. Daniel was different. His pear-shaped face, prominent chin, and round piercing eyes, coupled with his profound love of communicating, was attractive. He was the epitome of what a popular, athletic boy should look like. But athleticism was not a trait Daniel explored since elementary school.

Growing up, Daniel was never known for his athletic abilities. He was the last one to be picked for team sports and was often left out during recess games. Determined to prove himself, he decided to join the soccer team in the fifth grade. However, what followed was a series of disappointments and a valuable life lesson. Despite his efforts, Daniel struggled to keep up with the other players on the field. He lacked the speed and agility that seemed to come naturally for his teammates. Each time he played, he was met with disappointment.

His father had high hopes for Daniel to be more athletic like himself. As a result, Daniel found himself being benched often, feeling embarrassed and defeated. It was during this time that Daniel learned a valuable lesson: to only pursue things that he was naturally good at. The pressure to succeed and meet expectations had become too much for him to handle. He feared letting himself down. More importantly, he feared letting his parents down. He decided it was better to avoid anything that might lead to disappointment.

When Daniel was younger, he always looked up to his father. He admired his strong work ethic, his intelligence, and his unwavering determination to provide for their family. However, as he got older, he realized that his father's love and approval were not something that came easily. In fact, it seemed that no matter what he did, he could never meet his expectations. As a child, he was constantly seeking his father's approval. He strived to get good grades and be a model son. But no matter how hard he tried, his father always found something to criticize. He would point out every mistake, no matter how small. He never acknowledged his achievements. In fact, it seemed that no matter what Daniel did, he could never meet his expectations.

However, by middle school, Daniel traded in his soccer cleats for chinos and focused more on his academics. He excelled in his studies, earning him repeated placement on the honor roll board, membership in the Alliance for Excellent Education, and Early Academic Outreach Program. He finally found his pathway despite his father's constant disapproval because he just focused on academics.

"You need to get back into sports, Danny," Mr. Gardner would often say. "Every child, especially boys, need to play a team sport. It builds character and confidence."

Daniel would let his father's comments roll off his back. "You need to stop being a mama's boy and man up; playing sports does that."

Or the familiar: "So you think being a nerd is going to get you girls? Yeah, right!"

Daniel never liked sports and knew he would never be as good as his father in sports. So he focused on his passion for learning and embraced the secret praises he received from his mother while his father was at work.

It was no surprise that his mother, who affectionately called him her "Danny Bear," would wholeheartedly approve of his academic performance. She too was a scholar before settling into her duties as a housewife. Mrs. Gardner took pleasure in bragging about Danny and telling him how amazing he was but was reminded by Mr. Gardner that constant compliments ruined a man's character. So she left the praising and cute little name calling to when Mr. Gardner was not around.

After all, she had been calling him by this endearing nickname since the day he was born. But Daniel's entrance into this world was not an easy one for his mother. Her pregnancy had been difficult, and she had endured many challenges. Yet, as soon as her little Danny Bear arrived, weighing a healthy nine and half pounds, all those struggles seemed to disappear. He was a happy and cuddly baby boy, and his mother's love for him only grew stronger with each passing day. Throughout the years, Daniel continued to live up to his nickname. He was always a source of comfort and joy for his mother, who proudly watched him grow into the remarkable young man he was becoming.

His mother's reassurance of him becoming a great man was comforting for Daniel. Through his own self-discovery and reflection, Daniel realized that he did not have to conform to any specific stereotypes of masculinity. He learned that being a man was not about fitting into a predetermined mold but rather about being true to oneself and embracing his individual strengths and qualities. He also realized that there was no one way to be a man, and everyone's experience and expression of masculinity was unique.

Using his natural gifts to excel effortlessly in his studies while choosing his words wisely around his father made him a stellar son and student and became his own definition of a man. Daniel's personality only added to his already charming looks. He was confident, charismatic, and had a way with words that drew people toward him.

But there was still something missing with Daniel. A young boy navigating the complexities of adolescence, his desire for acceptance was especially strong. He longed to confide in someone about his innermost thoughts and feelings, but the fear of disappointing his parents and losing their love held him back. Daniel was a good student and well respected in his community. He had a loving family and was actively involved in his church. Yet, despite all of this, he felt a sense of emptiness inside. There was a nagging feeling that something was missing, and he couldn't quite put his finger on it. It seemed as though everyone around him had their life together, but he was struggling to make sense of his thoughts and emotions.

Now transferring to another school, Daniel was filled with a sense of excitement and eagerness for what lay ahead. One of the major advantages of relocating was the opportunity for a clean slate. In a new environment, people did not have preconceived notions or judgments about one's character. This provided Daniel with a chance to reintroduce himself and create a new persona that was free from the shadow of previous events. This was especially helpful for those who were recently caught in scandals back in Tennessee. Moving to a new place allowed him to break away from the negative associations and start afresh. This could help him focus on his personal growth and healing rather than constantly being reminded of the past.

This transfer marked a new chapter in his academic journey, and he was determined to make the most of it. He had spent the past few years finding and honing his strengths and weaknesses. Now, he was ready to show the world the version of himself that he wanted them to see.

Just like he was careful with the words with his dad, he was intentional with what he showed the world. First, it was crucial to recognize that this behavior was not a choice made from malice or selfishness. This was one of Daniel's superpowers, protecting himself from getting hurt again. Also, he feared vulnerability. It could paralyze him to be emotionally exposed. With much practice, he knew how to distance himself from those around him to avoid any potential pain or disappointment.

CHAPTER NINETEEN

Christmas morning came in like the wind, quick and taking me off guard. I could not believe how fast my time here in Chicago had flown by. It seemed like yesterday I was packing my bags and saying goodbye to Mama. Now I was reflecting on my time here, realizing that I was already nearing the end of my stay. There was a bittersweet feeling in my heart as I thought about leaving my family and this city behind. On the one hand, I was excited to see my besties and catch up with Daniel. But on the other hand, I had an amazing time making more memories with Daddy, Grandma, and Franky. As much as Mama and Auntie missed me, I knew that the other half of my family has missed me just as much. But I needed to get back to Coral Bluff and see why Daniel has not texted me back. I wanted to know where his head was since today was the day he planned to come out to his parents.

Just as my thoughts were about to take me down a rabbit hole, I heard a gentle knock on my door.

"Drea, are you up?" Daddy said softly through the door. "Yes, I'm up, Daddy. I'll be out in a minute."

"We are all waiting for you in the living room."

My room was drafty, and although I had on a full flannel pajama set on, I put on a robe for extra protection from the stiff coldness in Grandma's house.

By the time I walked to the living room, Franklin was sitting on the sofa next to Grandma while Daddy sat on the chair angled toward the television, watching his favorite spy, James Bond. Daddy was a sucker for mysteries and James Bond movies.

"Bout time you got your lazy butt up."

"Shut up, Franklin."

"We've been waiting on you for like an hour."

"Leave your sister alone," Daddy said, looking back and forth from the television.

But Franklin could not let it go. "You always take her side. If it was me, you would have given me a long speech about how men should never be late and keep a lady waiting."

"What's your problem?" "You."

"Me?"

"Yes, you. You always walk around like the world revolves around you."

"Oh, please, you're just mad because you're the family screw-up."

"Enough!" Grandma stood tall, her voice firm and sturdy. The intensity in her eyes could not be ignored as she spoke. Her words carried weight that demanded attention. It was clear that she meant business. "It's Christmas, and you two can't get along for one day? We are family and arguing with each other just further divides us." There was no doubt that she believed in what she was saying, and that belief was contagious.

"I'm sorry, Franklin. I'm sorry for keeping everyone waiting."

"Nah, my bad, little sister."

"I'm going to get breakfast started, and y'all go ahead and open the gifts." She kissed Franklin and me on our foreheads as she moved toward the kitchen.

After opening our gifts, eating breakfast, and watching the ending of Live and Let Die with Daddy, I returned to my room to relax. Curling back up under my warm covers, I reached for my phone to call Mama and wish her and Auntie Jolie a merry

Christmas. But I was late because I had already had four missed calls from Mama.

Holding my breath and hoping she was not upset at me for not calling her when I first woke up, I called her back.

"It's about time, missy. Merry Christmas." "Merry Christmas, Mama."

"So you're not dead. I've called you like three or four times. I even talked to Franklin this morning. What have you been doing?"

"I woke up late. Then we were opening gifts and ate breakfast."

"And you couldn't take a minute to call your mother? I've barely talked to you since you left last week."

"Daddy has been taking us out to different sites." "Like where?"

"We've been ice skating, went to ZooLights at Lincoln Park,
and stopped by Christkindmarket and Navy Pier."

Silence met me next on the phone. I did not know if I did not sound apologetic for not calling her earlier or if she were pissed that I had not called her since I landed last week.

"I see." She cleared her throat. "You two have been busy."

"Yes, ma'am. Remember we use to always go to Navy Pier when we visited grandma? Oh, wait, you remember that time when I first learned to ice skate and fell so hard I couldn't sit for a whole day?" I giggled, thinking about that memory.

"Yeah, I remember." Her voice was dry with a hint of sadness. "I just wanted to hear your voice and make sure you're okay. We are doing fine down here."

"Is Auntie still there?"

"Yes."

"Are you okay, Mama? Are you still mad at me?"

"No, Drea. Just don't forget about your mother. I do want to hear from you. But you go ahead and spend time with your father. I love you."

"Love you, too." I hung up as I felt disconnected from mama.

What was really bothering her? I thought adults always had the answer and would tell anyone how they feel. But my parents had now become so secretive with their feelings, I didn't know what was going on with my family.

I let the thoughts linger as I was committed to getting back warm. I nestled comfortably under my thick cotton covers. I suddenly heard feet walking down the hallway until it stopped in front of my door.

"Andrea."

"Hey, Grandma." I poked my head out from under the covers.

"Was that your mother?"

"Yes, ma'am. I wished her and auntie Jolie a merry Christmas."

"Your mother and aunt are so sweet. I miss them."

I did not know where this conversation was coming from or where it was going, but it felt like she wanted to talk.

"I didn't realize how much I would miss them," she continued. "Bianca is like the daughter I never had."

"Is everything alright, Grandma?"

She looked hesitant and walked over to my door and gently closed it. Walking back to my bed, she sat on the edge with her hands folded in her lap. "It's quite breezy in this old house. I need to get Shane to put more plastic around these windows to keep the chill out."

I did not say a word. I really did not know what to say. I just wanted to lay down under my covers and not come out until I absolutely had to.

"Andrea." "Yes, ma'am."

"I'm glad you're here. You and Franklin are growing up so fast. I still see you two as little kids running around playing with your new toys."

I giggled. "And now we argue over who is late to Christmas breakfast."

"Oh, he was just putting on. He's still trying to come into his manhood."

I hang onto her last word manhood because Franklin is eighteen but still acts like he is the annoying twelve-year-old brother. What exactly were these characteristics and traits that define manhood? Was it physical strength, emotional maturity, financial stability, or all the above? Would Daniel come into his manhood?

Would people in Coral Bluff look at him as a man?

"Look, I know this may be difficult for you," Grandma continued as she interrupted my thoughts. "The divorce and how you spend your holidays now."

"I mean, it is hard, but at least I still get to see y'all."

"Franklin had a hard time adjusting after the divorce." Her eyes wandered off. I could feel a sudden shift in the atmosphere when my grandmother brought up our family dynamics It caught me off guard. But I realized that she never finished her conversation about our family dynamics the other day before Daddy shut down the whole topic. But as she continued to speak, I understood that her intentions were pure and meaningful. "I can only imagine how you must feel."

"I don't know, some days are better than others. I just don't understand why. Why did they have to divorce? We were so happy." The thought of not knowing why my parents divorced sent a heat wave down my back, making me emerge from under the covers. "Mama never talks about it, and Auntie doesn't give me a straight answer. And Daddy doesn't discuss it either. It's like we were happy one day. Divorced the next day. And we all have to live with it."

"Divorce is never easy. It's a decision that comes with a lot of emotions and repercussions, and no one wants to go through it. In my humble opinion, they never should have gotten a divorce." She stopped, and the look on her face said she said too much. "I should not have said that. I'm sorry for talking about this with you."

"No. I'm old enough to know. I need to know what happened."

"That's just it. I'm not completely sure why they divorced.

Shane refuses to talk about it, even to this day. But I know they were in love with each other. I believe they still are in love with each other. A love like what they had never dies. It might get stale or grow old, but it never dies."

"So what then?"

"Only time will tell, honey, but just know you are loved by both of your parents. Sometimes adults complicate things that shouldn't be complicated. And they get so far down the road with who is right and not wanting to admit fault, a wedge is formed and slowly starts to separate them. You understand what I'm saying?"

Thinking back on the argument that almost destroyed Daniel and my friendship and how we both behaved, I completely understood. "Yes, ma'am. I understand."

"I love you, baby girl."

"I love you too, Grandma."

"You leave in a couple of days. Is there anything else you want to do before you leave?"

"No, not really. I forgot how cold the winters are here."

We both laughed, and she gave me the best warm hug.

Kissing me on my forehead, she said, "Get some rest. Your daddy is going to be in front of that TV watching every Bond movie for the rest of the day."

"Ha, I already know."

That was the first time anyone in our family addressed the topic of divorce. Laying back under the covers, the conversation had me thinking about relationships, whether romantic or friendship.

The drama and miscommunication Daniel and I experienced and the disagreements me, Harmony, and Noelle have were no different. If we could talk and overcome our differences, why cannot adults do the same? Why not Mama and Daddy?

CHAPTER TWENTY

Two weeks in the universe of school time would have taken forever, but when I was on vacation or having fun with friends or family, the time seemed to fly by. And now my time here in Chicago had come to an end, at least until the summer.

I packed my suitcase and felt a little sad that I was leaving.

When Franklin was not working, we were able to spend some sibling time together. He drove me around to places where he like to hangout after work and talk to girls. And I swear I had gained about ten pounds because Grandma cooked good food three times a day. I was really going to miss that. And my time with Daddy. His presence lit up my world, and I could not imagine my life without him. I was proud to call him my dad.

"You're just about ready, baby girl?" Daddy asked, walking into my room.

"Yep. I think I have everything. If I don't, I'll be back in a few months."

"This is your home too so you can leave whatever you like here."

I smiled at the thought of having two homes, but something just felt better with us living all under one roof. "Thanks, Daddy."

"Let me know when you're finished packing, and I'll put your suitcase in the car. No need to rush. We have a few hours before your plane leaves."

"I'm just about done, but I'll let you know."

My phone vibrating in my back pocket sent a rush of excitement into my heart. I hoped it was Daniel returning my text. I was disappointed; it was a Snapchat notification.

"Everything okay, honey?"

I forgot Daddy was still in the room. "Huh? Oh, yes. I just thought it was somebody else."

"Well, I'll let you get to it, and if you need anything, I'll be in the living room."

"Thanks, Daddy."

After he left, I sat on my bed, wondering why Daniel had not responded to any of my calls or texts since before Christmas. It took courage and strength to stand up for ourselves and our beliefs, especially when it involved revealing something personal about ourselves. I wanted to be there for him during this tough time.

I knew Daniel long enough to know that there was some fear in his last text that he was telling his parents about his sexuality on Christmas. He had mentioned before that he was worried about their reaction and the impact it would have on his relationship with them.

"I hope he's okay," I whisper to myself. I placed my phone in my back pocket and prepared to fly back to Alabama.

Six hours later, I was back in Coral Bluff. Mama and Auntie picked me up from the airport. I could tell they missed me, and it felt good to be missed. Walking back into my home and room brought back the familiar feeling of loneliness. It felt nice to have someone at home like it was in Chicago. No matter what time I woke up or despite the length of time Daddy and I stayed out sightseeing, I could count on Grandma being home with something cooking on the stove. Coming back to my house, I did not smell or see any traces of the kitchen that had been used today. And I knew Mama would not be home tomorrow when I woke up. That thought alone made me feel a little sad.

"Put your things down, and you can unpack later. You hungry? We can go to your favorite seafood spot." Mama was in a good mood, and she looked rested. I had not seen her smile that hard since the winter dance.

"No, I just want to get out of these clothes and relax."

"I'll run and pickup something for us to eat, and you can stay here with your aunt. That way we can stay in for the rest of the night."

"Yes, ma'am."

She skipped out of my room so happy like she just won some money and she was going to pick it up.

After my shower and putting on a fresh pair of pajamas, I went back to my room, lay across the bed, and babysat my phone. I thought Daniel would have sent some type of communication by now.

"I'm glad you had fun up there," Auntie Jolie said, walking into my room and making herself comfortable at my desk.

I put my phone down with Daniel in the back of my mind. I also remembered I had to text the girls too.

"Oh, I did. I love Chicago."

"Yeah, me too. It's such a beautiful city." "It's such a cold city."

"Yeah, it is." She played with her skirt, folding and unfolding the fabric on the seam. "How's your daddy?" "He's doing good. Everybody is doing good." "Did he ask about your mother?"

"No, not really. Grandma asked about y'all." "I've always liked Shane's mother. Sweet lady."

I wondered what Auntie really wanted. Whatever it was, I just hoped she didn't talk in riddles this time. I distracted myself by trying to pull a loose string I found on my pajama sleeve.

"I'll let you rest, and we'll catch up later."

"Okay, Auntie."

I reached for my phone, only to see more notifications. I texted the girls. I'm back!!

Harmony sent two thumbs-up emojis, and Noelle hearted the message. They both must be busy, but at least they acknowledged my message.

I decided to text Daniel one more time before I called it quits and just waited until I saw him at school on Monday.

Hey! I'm back home.

Bubbles appear. We need to talk. Can I come over?

Anxiety mixed with confusion rushed through my body.

Sure.

Suddenly, I was not as tired as I thought I was from traveling. I sprang into action, putting on some sweats in preparation for Daniel.

"Auntie, Daniel is going to stop by," I yelled out from my bedroom as I took off my hair bonnet and put my hair into a high ponytail puff.

"Right now?" her voice responded back from somewhere in the house. "You just got back." "He needs to talk." "Okay."

In the grand scheme of things, two weeks was not a long time to not consistently speak to someone. But when you are used to seeing and talking to someone every day and do not speak to them during those two weeks, it could feel like an eternity. That was how it felt for me while I anxiously waited for Daniel's arrival. I and the girls texted almost every day while I was gone, but the missed calls and the ignored messages made the distance with Daniel grow with each passing day. It was hard not to let my thoughts spiral into a state of worry and doubt, especially when I know he came out to his parents. What happened? What did his parents say? Did he get cold feet and not tell them? These questions weighed heavily on my mind, but I tried not to focus on them. Instead, I focused on making sure to keep an open mind.

A couple of hours later, the sun began to set, casting a warm orange light over the trees outside my bedroom window. My stomach grumbled in hunger. It had been a long day, filled with traveling and waiting for Daniel to stop by. Just as my thoughts turned to food, Mama came back carrying a bag from Happy's Chicken Shack. My excitement grew as I followed her into the kitchen, mouthwatering at the tantalizing smells floated from the bag.

"Sorry it took me so long. I had to run a few errands too." "I'm starving," I said as I eagerly grabbed a plate from the cupboard and watched as my mother unpacked the bag, revealing

perfectly crafted pieces of fried chicken. "Where's your auntie?"

"She's in the back."

"Go on and help yourself. I'll be back."

"Oh, Daniel is going to stop by."

"Now? I didn't get enough food for four people."

"I don't think he's staying for dinner. He just wanted to catch up."

"Are you sure you and Daniel are just friends? It seems to me that you two are more."

Of course she thought that. Everyone thought that we were more than friends except auntie because she knew the truth. But I was too hungry to explain our friendship. I was more excited to eat. I could not help but smile as I remembered the last time we had Happy's Chicken Shack. It was a family favorite, and just the thought of sinking my teeth into that crispy skin sent shivers of anticipation down my spine. "Mom, we are just friends. That's it."

"Okay. I won't mention another word about it. Did you wash your hands?"

"Yes, ma'am," I said, sitting down at the table. My phone vibrated and a text came through.

On my way.

It was Daniel, which meant I had at least fifteen minutes to dig into this chicken.

"Just put the rest of the food on the stove and your auntie and I will eat later."

I thumbed up Daniel's message as I sank my teeth into the chicken leg. "Yes, ma'am," I responded without looking up. I savored each bite. The chicken was cooked to perfection, crispy on the outside and tender on the inside. It was the kind of food that brought people together and created fond memories. Even Grandma would be pleased with this food.

A few moments later, the doorbell rang.

"Damn. It's been fifteen minutes. That's fast." I checked the time on my phone and more than twenty minutes had passed by.

Looking at the remains of my meal, I felt a sense of satisfaction. I looked at the evidence of grease and crumbs on my fingers. The smell of the rich, unhealthy meal lingered in the air, but I quickly snapped out of my trance and disposed of the bones. Without wasting any time, I walked over to the kitchen sink and rinsed off the plate. As I dried my hands and headed toward the front door, I wiped around my mouth, making sure there were no crumbs lingering around.

"What's up?" I asked when I opened the door and saw Daniel standing on my front porch.

"Hey." His voice was soft and timid. "Can we just sit out here on your porch? I can't stay too long."

"Sure."

Before closing the door, I said, "Mama, I'm outside with Daniel." I closed the door before I heard her response, eager to hear what Daniel had to say.

Daniel sat on our green and purple porch chair, and I sat across from him with my back toward the street. His khaki pants were amplified against the chair's vibrant colors.

I could see that he was lost in thought, his eyes unfocused and staring into the distance. "Long time no see or hear from you."

"Yeah."

"Well, how are you? Did you tell your parents?"

He took a deep inhalation and let out the biggest sigh I've ever heard. "Yeah, I told them."

"And>"

"They weren't happy. They're still not happy. I'm surprised they even let me come over here."

"Wait, what happened?"

"I finally told them I was gay during Christmas dinner. My mom started crying, and my dad got really mad and said no son of his is going to be a . . . "

"A what?"

He paused, and tears came rushing to his eyes, "A faggot." I'd never seen Daniel cry before. I quickly hugged him,

offering some type of support.

"My dad couldn't even look at me the next day. I felt so ashamed and unwanted," he said, crying into my shoulder.

"What about your mama?"

"She's following my dad's lead. She doesn't want to seem too affectionate toward me and upset my dad even more. I just feel so alone. That's why I didn't respond to your messages. I just didn't want to talk about it." He sat up and tried to dry off his tears with his sweater sleeve.

"Your parents may not like it, but at least you told your truth and got it off your chest."

"Nah. I think I've done more damage." "What do you mean? It's who you are."

Daniel got quiet and wiped off the rest of his tears. "I never told you why we moved to Coral Bluff."

"I figured your dad just got a new job."

"My father is a corporate attorney. You just don't get jobs on short notice like that anywhere."

"Well, how did he get a job at that big law firm downtown?" "My father is from here, and my mother is from Tennessee.

He met her in college up there and had me in Elkhorn. I got into a little bit of trouble last summer, and we moved back to my father's hometown for a new start."

"What type of trouble?"

I could see Daniel getting agitated. He rubbed his knees and inhaled and exhaled again. "My mother caught me masturbating to a picture of our neighbor. His son." He lowered his head and started to cry again. "She told my father." More tears streamed down his face, but he could not wipe them fast enough. "He questioned me for hours until I finally told him we kissed before."

"Oh, Daniel I'm so sorry." I hugged him again. "I'm so sorry you had to go through that."

He didn't say anything. His tears spoke volumes.

"Do you want to tell me what happened afterwards? You don't have to if you're uncomfortable."

"No, you make me feel safe." A gentle smile tried to appear on his face. "My father was enraged and went to our neighbor's father and told him everything I said. When they questioned the boy, he denied everything, saying I came on to him. It devastated me. I really cared about him. I thought he cared about me."

Silence filled the cool, dark evening. I felt a mixture of emotions, including sadness and concern. I wished his parents would have been more understanding and loving, accepting their son for who he was. Why are adults so fucked up?

"It was his loss. You're a great guy, and you shouldn't feel like you did anything wrong Daniel."

"But why do I? I feel like I don't belong, like an outcast. Why?"

"People are stupid, especially adults. They pretend they have our best interest in mind, but they really don't." "Yeah."

"I hate you had to go through that, but I am so happy I met you."

"Yeah. Me too."

"It's getting chilly. You're sure you don't want to come in?"

"Nah. I have to get going anyway. My dad only let me out the house because I was going to see a girl." He rolled his eyes. "My parents are so backwards. They thought moving here would instantly make me straight."

"I think a lot of parents are backwards. But will you be able to talk when you get home?"

"Probably through text. I don't want them to hear our conversations."

"Are you sure you're okay?" "Yeah. Thanks for listening." "I'll always be here."

Daniel finally was able to manage a genuine smile. "I know, and I appreciate you."

I knew my friend needed someone to lean on, someone who would listen without judgment and offer a shoulder to cry on. And I was glad to be that person for him. As long as we were in Coral Bluff, Daniel would continue to navigate this new chapter in his life, and I would stand by his side, offering my judge free support and love. Because at the end of the day, love knew no boundaries or limitations. My friend deserved to be loved and accepted for who he is, and I would do everything in my power to make sure he knew it.

CHAPTER TWENTY-ONE

It had been a couple of weeks since Daniel and I had our heartfelt conversation on my porch. He truly opened up to me, and I was able to see yet another side of him. His vulnerability was sad, but I felt like I needed to be there for him. But I was not sure if he felt the same way about our conversation. It felt like he was shutting me out again. He was shutting everyone out. He seemed to have withdrawn from social interactions and kept to himself during school. In fact, I rarely saw him talking to anyone or even participating in class. We barely talked during class too. I was not even sure where he went during lunch. He did not eat with me or anyone from our class anymore. And he would disappear right after the last bell.

Something had changed in him. Yes, he still dressed nice and smelled deliciously good, but it seemed like he was just going through the motions of coming to school. I missed walking home with him to work on our project and telling silly jokes about our classmates. I knew he was going through some things at home, but this was different; something was different.

His usual cheerful demeanor had been replaced with a sense of detachment. He appeared to be content with his own company and avoided any kind of social interaction. One time after school, Daniel disappeared without saying a word. I tried to start up casual conversations with him by his locker, but he simply smiled politely and left without giving me any indication of where he was headed. This had further fueled my curiosity about his sudden isolated behavior. And while it was normal for people to have days when they preferred to keep to themselves, Daniel's behavior had been consistent for weeks now. This was concerning because he used to be such a sociable person.

Until that wet, rainy Wednesday morning, I and the girls slushed our way, avoiding puddles, to school. I wore my favorite yellow raincoat. I could not help but smile every time I wore it. The bright color stood out against the gloomy backdrop. The raincoat was gifted from my mama a few years ago, and it had been my go-to attire for rainy days ever since. It might sound silly, but somehow this simple raincoat always managed to bring a sense of cheerfulness to my day. As well as keeping me dry and protected from the relentless raindrops.

"God, I can't wait until the weekend," Noelle said, bunching her hair into her hood so the few curls she had left could last. "Is it me or does this semester seem to be going by slow as hell?"

"Yeah, it is going by slow. But I think you noticed more because football season is over," Harmony said with a giggle.

"Yeah, maybe so. I don't have anything to look forward to. I mean, I still have responsibilities as captain, but I'm bored."

"Why didn't you cheer during basketball season? That would make the second semester go by faster."

Noelle sucked her teeth. "I hate basketball."

"Girl, you ain't got to play the damn sport. You're just cheering on the players."

"Cheering is much more than that. It's a whole sport." "A sport?"

"Yes, Harmony, a sport!"

"Yeah, okay, if you say so. Drea, you're pretty quiet over there."

"I didn't want to interrupt y'all's debate over cheerleading." "Ha ha. Very funny. She's probably quiet because she hasn't

been hanging out with her boyfriend, Daniel."

"For the millionth time, Noelle, Daniel is not my boyfriend."

"Well, why y'all haven't been hanging out?"

"I don't know. I mean, he's been busy and so have I." "Cap!" Harmony said as we sped up our pace to cross the street to get into the building. "You haven't been that busy. Not so much you couldn't hang out with Daniel."

"I'm not capping. In fact, we're hanging out after school today." Why did I say that? I hadn't really spoken to Daniel let alone hung out with him in weeks.

"Oh, really?" Harmony said, taking off her hood as we entered school. "So you're not walking home with us today?"

"Nah, but I'll text y'all later." "Uh-huh. Okay."

Out of the three of us, Harmony was always the suspicious one. I didn't know if that trait was developed after she became a mother, but ever since she had Matthew, she could always tell when someone was lying, especially me.

"I'll see y'all later," I said, throwing up my hands and slinging water from the sleeve of my raincoat on the floor. I was more concerned about how I would get Daniel to hang out with me today. Besides, me and Daniel were friends. He was just going through some things right now.

I saw Daniel at his locker, and I knew this was my chance to talk to him before class started. And since I did not see him during lunch anymore and he vanished after school, I did not know when I would have another time to talk to him.

I gathered up all my strength and walked toward him. "You look very nice in your rain jacket."

My efforts were stopped short when Oliver cut in front of me, smiling ear to ear.

"Oh! Hey, Oliver." "Did I scare you?"

"No, I was just going to—"

"Going to what? Go and talk to your boyfriend?" he says, pointing down the hallway toward Daniel.

"What? No! I was going to my locker, silly. And I told you, he's not my boyfriend."

"I'll walk with you to your locker." "Oh, you don't have to."

"But I want to. I've barely talked to you. I feel like everything has changed between us since we kissed."

"Oliver, nothing has changed."

"You've been avoiding me, and you know it."

Getting my first set of books out of my locker and feeling annoyed, I said, "No, I have not. I went to Chicago for two weeks."

"You've been back for weeks now. Plus, I texted you over the break with no response. If you don't fuck with me like that, just say it."

I was getting nervous and anxious. The last bell before the late bell just rang; I was being questioned by Oliver, and I had yet to speak with Daniel.

"Oliver, you're a nice guy—" "But."

"There's no but. You're a nice guy, and let's catch up because I have been busy."

"Really? When?"

"How about this Friday after school? We can check out that new ice cream spot on the corner of fifth and Langley."

"It's a date."

"It's not a date. We are just hanging out."

"Whatever you want to call it. I'll see you then."

Letting out the biggest sigh, I hurried to first period. Walking into class, I saw Daniel sitting in the back of class. There was an empty seat next to him, and I took it.

"Hey."

He nodded while doodling on the outside of his notebook.

Whispering as low as I could, I said, "Why have you been avoiding me?"

Daniel looked at me like I had three heads. He shrugged his shoulders and continued to draw. "We need to talk."

"Alright, class. Let's get settled into our seats so we can start," Mrs. Holmer said from in front of the board.

I sat back in my seat, feeling embarrassed. I felt like Oliver must have felt when I avoided him. And just then, Daniel slipped me a note.

Let's talk after class.

I nodded and felt a slight smile come on my face.

I was rehearsing what I would say in my head when the bell rang. Everyone but Daniel and I took our time getting up and walking to our next class.

"Daniel, what's going on with you? You've disappeared yet again after you came over." As I was saying everything I rehearsed in my head, I noticed a gold cross around Daniel's neck. "What is that?"

"What?"

Pointing to the gold chain, I said, "This thing around your neck. I've never seen it before."

"I got it at church."

"Oh. Well, where have you been? Why don't you talk to me?"

"There's a lot of shit going on."

"Talk to me. Are we or are we not friends?"

He paused, searching for that answer. "You're right. We are friends."

"So stop cutting me out, Daniel. It's not fair." "No, you're right. Let's talk after school." "You want to come over to my house?"

"No, you have to come over to mine. My parents want me to come straight home after school."

"Why?"

"Long story but can you come over?"

"Yeah. I'll just text my mom and let her know."

After walking into our second period class, the knots in my stomach seemed to disappear.

"Drea." Daniel said with grief in his eyes. "Yeah?"

"Thank you for being patient with me."

"What do you mean?"

"Alright, class, take your seats. We have a lot to cover today," Mrs. Lee said as she interrupted our conversation that lingered from last period.

I counted down the time when school would be over. It always felt like the time goes by super slow when you are trying to do something or go somewhere and goes by super-fast when you are having fun. But today, time went by fast enough to go through our seven classes and head to Daniel's house.

Walking back with Daniel to his house felt like old times again. The only thing that was missing was the sense of urgency to complete Mr. Fitzgerald's project.

"Thank God it stopped raining," I said, still wearing my raincoat.

"Yeah, it would suck if we had to walk back in the rain."

"So what's been up with you? You disappeared during winter break after you told me you came out to your parents. Then you came to my house and spilled out your guts to me. And now you've been avoiding me like I have COVID or something."

"There's been a lot of stuff going on." "Daniel, I'm your friend. Don't you trust me?" "You're right, and I'm sorry."

"Did you get into trouble when you went back home the day you left my house?"

"Nah, not really. My parents are making me go to this church thing every weekend now."

"Every weekend?"

"Yeah. And the pastor gave me this necklace. He says it will protect me from having impure thoughts about other men."

I could not help but laugh, which made Daniel laugh. We were both laughing uncontrollably. The more we laughed, the more we found the whole idea hilarious.

"Wait, wait. You mean your pastor told you that a necklace with a cross will keep you from being who you're meant to be?"

"Yeah, I guess." "And you believe it?"

"Of course not. I'm just trying to make my parents happy." "And what about you? Are you happy?"

He stopped laughing. I stared at the sudden change of his expressions, it was alarming and made me feel uneasy.

"It makes me feel like something is wrong with me."

"What do you mean?"

"I mean, why do I like what I like? Why am I attracted to men and not women?"

"I don't know, but it doesn't make you less of a person. Hell, it doesn't even make you different."

"Yeah, well, it doesn't feel that way."

"Maybe it's not you that needs to change. Maybe it's your parents and pastor who need to change."

Silence fills the cool, wet air again. And then Daniel says, "Can I tell you something?"

"Of course."

"I've been seeing someone."

I stopped walking and pulled his arm back to make him stop too. "What? Who? Do I know him?" "Maybe. Promise you won't tell." "I promise."

"Not even Harmony and Noelle."

"I didn't even tell them you are gay. They still think we are together."

"Really?"

"That's not the point. Who are you talking to?"

He took a big inhale and exhaled slowly. "Christopher Jacobs."

"Christopher Jacobs? The football player?" "Yeah," he says, blushing.

"Isn't he like a senior?"

"He's a junior."

"Is that why you've been disappearing during lunch and after school?"

"Maybe," he said with a devilish grin. "How did this happen?"

"I met him at church."

"Church? Of all the places."

"We are both part of this group to help teens live a more 'holy life.'" He uses air quotes as he explains. "We started talking after the meetings, and we just clicked."

"You seem really happy when you talk about him." "I'm just taking my time. I've been hurt before." "Well, your secret is safe with me."

"Maybe one day we can double date with you and Oliver," he said, laughing again.

"Oh, you got jokes," I said, pinching the back of his arm. "But for real, he is really into you."

"Yeah. Oliver is cool, but he wants a relationship." "What's wrong with that?"

"I don't know. I guess I would rather focus on school than on a relationship."

"Why can't you do both?"

"Wait a minute. Weren't we talking about you and Christopher?"

"Yeah, about us double dating."

"There won't be any double dates, but I am hanging out with him this weekend."

"Really? So you do like him?"

"I never said I didn't like him. I just don't want a relationship."

"Good for you, Drea. I wish I could go out with Christopher on a date without being judged."

"One day you will. One day we will both move away from this place and live in a place where people won't judge you for being yourself."

"Does that place exist?"

"Sure, it does. There's lots of places like that."

We arrived at Daniel's house. Our catch-up conversation was so interesting, I did not realize we were even in his neighborhood.

Walking into his house was still as impressive as ever with its intricate design. However, when I stepped inside, it felt colder and more unloved. It was hard to pinpoint exactly what had changed, but the air felt heavy and uninviting. The walls that were once adorned with family portraits and vibrant paintings now stood bare, as if they were hiding some dark secrets. The furniture that used to be carefully arranged in every room now seemed scattered and neglected.

"Where are your family photos?" I whispered, walking closely behind Daniel. If his parents were home, I didn't want them to hear my intrusive question.

"My dad took them down." "But why?"

He shrugged his shoulders. I could sense his mood had changed from the carefree laughing Daniel to an uptight, unavailable Daniel. I liked the former Daniel.

"Daniel, is that you?" his dad's voice called out from the back room.

"Yes, sir. And Drea is here too."

I finally reached the kitchen, and even though it was still spacious and beautiful, it lacked the coziness and charm that I remembered. Daniel grabbed two bottles of apple juice from the refrigerator.

"Here you go." "Thanks."

Seconds later, I heard feet walk toward the kitchen. They walked in with a concerned look on their faces like they had to see me for themselves.

"Hello, Drea," Mrs. Gardner said, looking royal as usual next to Mr. Gardner. The cream pantsuit she wore was immaculate, hugging her figure and highlighting her graceful posture. The color was a subtle yet powerful choice, giving sophistication and confidence. Its simplicity allowed her natural beauty to shine through. But it was her choice of lip color that truly captured my attention. The boldness of the red against the creamy backdrop of her outfit added a touch of glamour and elegance to her overall appearance. Her poise and clothes made her stand out from the women in this town who thought leggings and scrubs were the normal clothes of choice unless there was a special occasion. "We haven't seen you in a while."

"I was visiting my family in Chicago over the break."

"Yes, I believe Daniel mentioned that. Would you like something else to drink?"

"No, ma'am. This apple juice is fine."

His dad did not say anything as Mrs. Gardner led the conversation. Daniel was fidgeting with the top to his apple juice container, avoiding eye contact with either of his parents.

Mrs. Gardner continued, "How was school, Daniel?"

"Did you do what the pastor said to do throughout the day?" his dad interjected, ignoring Mrs. Gardner's previous question. There was a certain sense of authority that radiated from his dad. It was as if his posture and demeanor were specifically designed to command attention and respect. With his stern expression and firm voice, it was evident that he was not a person to be trifled with. His face seemed to reflect the depth of his character. His brow was wrinkled, and his jaw was set. But it was not just his appearance that was imposing; it was his voice as well. He did not speak often, but when he did, every word was enunciated with precision and purpose. The tone of his voice was firm. It was apparent that this man was not one to gloss over his words or sugarcoat the truth. He spoke with a straightforwardness that demanded attention. There was no room for uncertainty in his words.

"Yes, sir."

"How many times?"

"I don't know. A lot I guess." Daniel was becoming more annoyed.

Mr. Gardner finally acknowledged me and said, "Chicago, huh?"

"Yes, sir." My voice sounded shaky. I did not know why I was nervous, but his dad seemed to have that effect on people.

"I've been there several times. Never really liked it though. It's too liberal and cold."

I did not know what to say so I sipped on my apple juice. "Are you two hungry?" Mrs. Gardner asked, trying to redirect the conversation.

Before either one of us could answer, Mr. Gardner asked, "Who stays up there?"

"My father, brother, and grandmother." "And what does your father do for work?" "He's a history teacher."

"A teacher, huh? That's a noble profession."

Mrs. Gardner looked uncomfortable, shifting her weight from one side to the next. Daniel refused to look up at anyone, and I was uncomfortable with his line of questioning and shady ass remarks about my daddy's city. But I bit my tongue and said nothing.

"Are you staying for dinner?"

"No, sir. My mama is expecting me to be home soon."

His eyes shifted from me to Daniel to back to me again. It was like he was trying to read us.

"Well, there's a seat at our table for you. Hopefully you can come over more often. It seems that he needs to be around more girls anyway." Mr. Gardner said motioning toward Daniel.

Again, the room fell silent. There was a sense of unease that seemed to settle over all of us. The atmosphere was tense and awkward, and it was evident that no one knew how to act or what to say. I could feel the tension radiating from everyone, including Mrs. Gardener. It was clear that something was not right, but no one seemed willing to address it. I could sense that Mrs. Gardener was just as uncomfortable as Daniel and I, but she remained composed and quiet. Her usual warm and welcoming demeanor was replaced with a distant and guarded expression. It was evident that she was not going to say anything, and that only added to the unease in the room.

Finally, after what seemed like sixty seconds too long of silence, Daniel said, "We have some homework to finish so we'll be upstairs."

Although we did not have any homework, I was happy he broke up the silence. I followed Daniel up to his room where he plopped on the bed, and I sat at his desk.

"What was that about?" I said, pointing toward his bedroom door.

"That's just how my dad is: a fucking asshole." "Daniel."

"What? He's always been like that. I guess that character flaw is what makes him a great lawyer." He paused while he traced the checkered design on his comforter. "Sometimes my mother will spend all day preparing a meal for him. And when he gets home, he decides to go out to dinner instead, not even acknowledging my mother's hard work." He punched the bed. I thought he secretly wished it were his father's face. But he continued, "Or when he purchased that handgun he keeps in their closet. My mother hates guns, especially since her younger brother was shot to death when they were teenagers. But do you think my father cares about it? Fucking bastard."

"Oh, Daniel. I know you're upset, but don't call your dad out of his name."

"Why not? He's a fucking bully. And my mom is so weak; she won't say anything to him. She doesn't even stand up for herself. I hate them both."

"Don't say that. You only have one mama and one daddy." "Well, I want new ones."

I could feel the anger roaring from Daniel as he stared at the floor.

"Two more years."

Looking up at me, he asked, "What?"

"Two more years. Every time my mama gets on my nerves, I just remind myself that I won't always be in her house. I started counting down after my daddy left."

"Two years, huh?" "Yep. Two more years."

CHAPTER TWENTY-TWO

Daniel and I giggled as we passed notes to each other. They were short comments back and forth on who he would take to the spring dance. There was a joy and lightheartedness that radiated between us. It was evident in the way we giggled as we exchange words on a mere piece of paper. Our friendship started out rocky, and at times, I did not think we could come back from certain actions and statements. But now our friendship was built on a foundation of shared laughter and inside jokes. It was also grounded in mutual respect and understanding, which is why we were able to communicate with each other, even through something as simple as note passing. We had developed a special kind of language that only we could understand. It was filled with coded messages and cryptic drawings that held meanings known only to us. Sometimes, Harmony and Noelle felt left out because I spent more time with Daniel. I had to always remind them that Daniel and I had every class together. Besides, no one or nothing would ever disrupt our girl-power friendship of seven plus years.

Glancing at the clock, I knew school was almost over, and we would have an extended weekend celebrating Easter. But I also had my date with Oliver today. Daniel slid me another note, and I felt my phone vibrate in my pocket. Trying not to draw attention to myself, I discreetly took it out and saw a message from Oliver.

Meet me in the back of the school next to the teachers parking lot.

I quickly texted back, Ok.

Daniel cleared his throat, waiting on me to read his last note.

I read it and had to cover my mouth to keep me from laughing out loud and getting us both in trouble. Before I could write back, the bell rang. Every student dashed toward the door before Mrs. Drapper could assign any history work over the break.

"So who were you texting?" Daniel asked, gathering up his books into his book bag.

"Oliver."

"Ah, I see. Your boo."

"Oh, come on. He's not my boo."

"Okay then. Tell me this, what are you doing after school?" "Oh, shut up," I said, pinching him.

"Ow. Why do you always pinch me?"

"Because you deserve it."

Laughing because he knows I'm right, he said, "I'm meeting him over the weekend."

"Christopher?"

"Shh. Not so loud. But yep."

"Where? How? I mean, what are you telling your parents?" "After our meeting at church tomorrow, we are going back to his place. His parents are out of town."

"And your parents?"

"What about them?"

"What did you tell them you were doing after church? You know they want to know your every move."

"Oh, I told them that I'm hanging out with you." He flashed a devilish smile.

"Well, thanks for letting me know just in case they call looking for you."

"Thanks, Drea. You're the best." "Oh, I know."

"Have fun this evening."

"And you have fun tomorrow, but not too much."

"Can't promise that," he said, walking out of class.

I went to the bathroom to give myself a once-over. My fresh cornrows were popping, and I looked cute in my black denim and flannel shirt. I made sure nothing was in my teeth, and I headed toward the meeting place.

My heart started to race as I got closer and saw Oliver waiting for me. The cool air did not keep the palms of my hands from sweating.

"Hey, Drea."

"Hey."

"You ready?"

"Yeah, let's go. I've been wanting to check out this spot for a minute."

"Yeah, me too. But before we go, do you mind walking somewhere with me?"

"Where?"

"It's a surprise."

"I don't know. Besides, I hate surprises." "Really, Drea? You don't trust me?" "Yeah, I guess."

He looked offended when I said that. His eyes got wide, and he took a step back. "You guess?"

"Yeah, I trust you boy. Come on because I want my ice cream."

Five minutes later, we arrived at an abandoned building.

Vibrant colors of graffiti covered the side of the building. "Oliver, why are we at the old Sears building?" "Oh, come on. Let's explore."

"Explore? Why?"

"Why not?"

"Because it's been abandoned before either one of us was born."

"But it has so much history, and I thought a smart girl like yourself would appreciate the history of this place."

"What kind of history?"

"Just follow me."

I let out a big sigh as I rolled my eyes at him. We stepped inside. The musty smell of decay hit us, making us wrinkle our noses. Yet the captivating artwork on the walls kept us from turning back. The talent and creativity of the graffiti murals were evident in every stroke. We made our way through the corridors; I wondered about the building's history. Why did Sears go out of business? And why hasn't another business scooped this place up? It was in a prime location.

The cracked windows and peeling paint on the walls only added to the mysterious atmosphere of the place where my mother said she used to shop when she first moved to Coral Bluff. Despite its run-down appearance, the building exuded a sort of charm that drew us in further. We climbed up a flight of stairs and found ourselves on the rooftop, offering a breathtaking view of the city.

"Isn't this beautiful?" Oliver said, opening his arms out as if he were giving me the city as a gift.

"Oh, wow. This is breathtaking." "I told you."

"How did you know about this?"

"My mama worked here while she was in high school, and my dad proposed to her right here." "On the rooftop?"

"Uh-huh. My daddy always told me that story so I wanted to see it for myself. He brought me here last year, and it took my breath away."

"Oh, that's so romantic. Your parents have been married since high school?"

"Nah, they got married after they graduated from college. He just wanted to take my mother off the market," he said, laughing.

"Well, I think that is sweet and romantic."

"That's why I wanted you to see it. I asked you before if you would be my girlfriend, and you said no. So I'm asking again." He paused. "Will you be my girlfriend?"

I felt butterflies flying around in my stomach, moving up toward my throat. I swallowed hard to push them back down. My hands were shaking, and my heart was beating a mile a minute. I knew this feeling too well, and I did not like it. I felt overwhelmed.

"I don't know what to say."

His eyes were piercing my soul, and I could not look away from him. I knew there was a connection between us, but I was not sure if I wanted to explore that right now. But if not now, when?

Ugh! This was when I need my besties. I was so confused and nervous.

"Say yes."

Biting my bottom lip, I said, "Can I think about it?"

He let out a sigh, and his shoulders dropped down like he just lost his best friend. "Drea." "Yeah?"

"I really like you. I've never liked a girl as much as I like you. Plus, your father really likes me, and that's important."

Really? He was going to bring my daddy into the conversation again? That was a low blow, and he knew how much I respected my daddy's opinion.

"Yeah, you're right." "So?"

"Yeah, I guess so."

"Really? You're my girlfriend?" Oliver started jumping up and down and screaming, "Drea Ramsey is my girlfriend!"

"Shh! Shh! Shut up. You're so embarrassing."

"Drea," he said, panting like a dog and smiling from ear to ear. "Can I kiss you?"

"Kiss me?" "Yeah, kiss you."

"If I say yes, can we leave and go get ice cream?"

"I promise," he said, raising his right hand to the sky.

"Okay. Yes, you can kiss me."

The cool breeze brushed against our skin, sending shivers down my spine. I felt like I was in a movie with him as my leading man. He licked his lips and took a closer step toward me. And as I looked into his convincing eyes, time seemed to stand still. I could not help but get lost in the rhythm of his heartbeat, beating in sync with mine. He pulled my body close, tilted his head, and gently kissed my lips. It started off with a peck and graduated to his tongue going into my mouth. It was like fireworks exploding in my heart, igniting every inch of my being. His hand traveled up my back, pulling me in closer into him. And with each kiss, I could feel the intensity of our connection grow stronger.

His hands were resting on my waist, and the warmth of his touch was electric. I could sense his excitement building up as our kisses became more and more passionate. But then, I stopped. I felt a bit nervous as his desire became evident through his pants.

"I think that's enough," I said, pulling back.

"I'm so sorry, Drea. I didn't mean to offend you."

I could feel his disappointment, but I could not ignore my own feelings. I needed to feel comfortable and in control before taking things any further.

"You didn't offend me, but I do think it's time for ice cream." "You're right. Let's go get some ice cream."

I had never had a boyfriend before, but I was glad that my first one was Oliver. He was caring and never gave up on pursuing me since the second grade. And he was right; my daddy absolutely adored him. But I did not think I will tell daddy we had kissed just yet.

Arriving at Scoop It Up ice cream parlor, I pushed open the glass door and a sweet, creamy aroma immediately surrounded me. The scent of ripe strawberries and freshly churned cream tickled my nose and ignited my taste buds. The colorful display of various flavors and toppings invited me in, like a seductive siren luring me toward delicious temptation. The quaint interior of the parlor with its pastel-colored walls and vintage decor exuded a whimsical charm.

Soft music played in the background, adding to the romantic atmosphere. I thought that I was going on a romantic date, straight out of one of those classic movies Grandma watched when Daddy was not watching sports or James Bond.

Smiling staff members in crisp, white uniforms eagerly greeted me. Their eyes twinkled with anticipation of satisfying my craving for a frozen treat. As I made my way to the counter, I was met with an array of options that made my heart skip a beat. From classic flavors, like chocolate and vanilla, to more exotic choices, like toasted coconut and mint chocolate chip, each one looked more tempting than the last.

"Hello! May I take your order?" A girl behind the counter asked me. She looked to be my age, smiling from ear to ear.

"I would like one scoop of cookie dough and one scoop of cookies and cream."

"Bowl or cone?" She followed up after my request. "Bowl."

"And for you, sir?" "I'll get the same."

I found us a table while Oliver paid for our ice cream. As I sat down, I felt grateful for this moment. I actually had a boyfriend. Wait until I tell the girls and Daniel the news. And what better way to spend our first date than over a scoop of my favorite sweets, ice cream?

Oliver returned with our ice cream bowls, and my excitement grew even more. I could not wait to dig in and taste the familiar flavors that always comforted me. We took a moment to capture the perfect Instagram-worthy picture of our treats, and then we finally took that first delicious bite.

"How is it?" Oliver said as he managed to talk without dropping ice cream from his mouth.

I could only nod in approval. The creamy texture and the burst of flavors in my mouth made me close my eyes and savor the moment. I could sense that Oliver was enjoying his ice cream just as much as I was. I was content and happy. The simple act of eating ice cream together felt like the most romantic thing in the world. And in that moment, I was grateful for Oliver, for this perfect evening.

"I will definitely come back here," I said, digging into my cookies and cream scoop. "And thank you for the ice cream."

"No problem."

"Did you use your allowance?"

Chuckling with the spoon in his mouth, he said, "No, I work part time."

Shocked by his ability to go to school and work, I had to know more. "You do? Where? Since when?"

"My mom was able to get me into the YLW program through the mayor's office. I've been in the program since last year." "What's YLW?"

"Youth Learn and Work. It helps build your skills and confidence to prepare you for life after high school. You also get placed at different work sites. And I've met so many people from different schools in this program."

"Wow, I guess Daddy was right. You are resourceful. I've never even heard of that program."

"Do you ever go by the information board, or do you just go to class and go home?"

Embarrassed by that his question exposed my lack of diversity in activities in and out of school, I shyly answered, "More of the latter."

"Drea, I know you're brilliant and you're taking those honor classes, but you have to be well-rounded. Colleges want to see that, not just your grades."

"Yeah, I guess you're right. When did you become so smart?"

"I've always been smart. You just never noticed."

"Make me feel bad, why don't you?"

"My bad. I don't want you to feel no type of way." "Thanks," I said with a hint of resentment.

Growing up, I always thought that being smart was enough to guarantee success. My parents constantly praised my intelligence and encouraged me to excel academically. So I did not bother with extracurricular activities or explore other interests outside of the classroom. If I could solve complex math problems and ace exams, I believed that doors would open for me. But now I was realizing that being smart was just one piece of the puzzle. Colleges were not only looking for academic excellence but also for well-rounded individuals with diverse experiences.

"Get out of your head," Oliver said, smiling from across the table.

"What?"

"I can see you over thinking. Get out of your head. You're super smart and you're going to go to college, Drea."

"I know that. In fact, I'm going to go to The University of Chicago or Northwestern University."

"To be closer to your dad?"

"Yeah. Plus, they are great schools."

"Yeah, I've heard. You're finished with your ice cream?" "Yep."

"I'll walk you home. I have to be at my worksite by six-thirty p.m."

"Oh yeah. Let's get out of here."

We found ourselves walking back to my house, lost in laughter and flirtatious banter. The air was becoming chillier, but the warmth of our conversation kept us cozy. There was a certain magic in the air. It was rare to have such a carefree evening with someone I was beginning to develop feelings for.

"So, the spring dance," he said, grabbing my hand.

I playfully pulled my hand back. "What about the dance?" "Would you be my date?"

I hesitated to answer him because the girls and I already planned on going together and I just included Daniel today when we were passing notes in class.

"Um, I kinda already have plans." "You do? With who?"

"Harmony and Noelle said we are all going together since Harmony wasn't able to go to the winter dance."

"Oh, okay. I thought you were going to say you were going with Daniel."

"Why would you think that?"

"Because you two are always together. It's just weird." "He's one of my really good friends, and we take every class together."

"Yeah, but I still don't like it."

I did not want to push the issue as we got closer to my house. I did not want to tell him that Daniel was coming with the girls and me to the dance. I did not feel like telling him that we were planning to coordinate our outfits and walk in fashionably late. I bit my tongue and said, "Daniel and I are just friends."

"I know, I know. And I believe you."

As we neared my house, I was a little disappointed that our walk was coming to an end. But, as we reached my front porch, I could not suppress the smile that spread across my face.

"Thank you again for the ice cream."

"You're good," he said, leaning in for another kiss. Scared Auntie Jolie might be watching, I gave him a peck and a hug.

I went inside to relish the thought of me and Oliver.

I had a boyfriend.

CHAPTER TWENTY-THREE

The winter coldness began to blow away, and flowers started to bloom. When the first hint of spring popped out, everyone at Oak Valley High knew the spring dance was approaching. While the winter dance may have been a hit or miss for some, the spring dance was a highly anticipated event that captured the attention of the whole school.

There was something about the warmer weather and the promise of blooming flowers that made everyone want to bust out their dancing shoes and hit the dance floor. Unlike the winter dance, the spring dance was the one event that no one wanted to miss. The spring dance was like an unofficial kickoff party for the season of sunshine and warmth. And let us not forget about fashion. While the winter dance required fancy dresses and suits, the spring dance gave us a chance to let loose and have some fun with our outfits. Floral prints, pastel colors, and flowy dresses were all staples of spring dance fashion. It was a chance to show off our personal style and embrace the colors of the season. Another thing that set the spring dance apart from other school events was the atmosphere. There was just a sense of excitement and joy in the air. Everyone was happy to see the end of another school year approaching, and we were looking forward to summer break. It was a time for friends to come together, dance, and make memories before everyone went their separate ways for the summer.

"Mom, where is my purple and gold earrings?" I screamed from my room. I had managed to turn my room into a disaster zone with clothes, shoes, and purses all over. I was running behind, and I hadn't started my puff, bubble updo. "Ma."

"What?"

"Where are my gold and purple earrings?" "How am I supposed to know?"

Her rude response further irritated me. "Ugh! I wish Auntie Jolie was here," I whispered under my breath. She always knew what to do and say in times of distress. Plus, she knew where everything was hiding, unlike Mama. Mama was not home long enough to notice something went missing.

Auntie left for the weekend to go back to New Orleans. She said she had to make some money if she wanted to enjoy her vacation with us a little while longer. Auntie did not have a traditional job like Mama and Daddy. Auntie Jolie was a psychic reader and helped all types of people. Mama always said Auntie was blessed with the ability to see things before other people, but that used to get her into a lot of trouble when they were kids. I guess one of their neighbors didn't appreciate a seven-year-old telling his wife that he was cheating on her with her own cousin. But now she could make money from her abilities. I wish she could see people over Zoom rather in person. Either way, I still wish she were here to help me get ready for this dance.

"Crap! Let me just get dressed so I can do my hair." I continue to coach myself, "Come on, Drea. You got this."

My phone buzzed.

"Oh, great. That's probably the girls letting me know they're on their way."

To my surprise, it was Daniel letting me know he was headed to my house.

"Okay, I have at least fifteen to twenty minutes before he gets here. Let's just hope Noelle is running behind too."

Starting my bubble updo, I carefully sectioned off my hair, starting from the nape area, and discreetly placed rubber bands around each puff to hold it in place. I was prepared for this style. I had YouTubed this style a thousand times and practiced it every day for the last week, perfecting it. And tonight, it only took me one try to get it right.

My admiration was short lived when I looked at the clock and realized it was already seven o'clock. The dance started at six and ended at eleven. We all agreed we would be fashionably late but still had time to dance and show off our fits. Going through my closet, I quickly pulled out my gold, strapless, sequined dress.

My heart skipped a beat. It was absolutely perfect. I could not believe my mom bought it for me since she mocked at it in the store, saying it was to mature for me. The way it hugged my size- two figure was simply perfect. I had been eyeing this dress for weeks, but I could not justify spending that much money on it. But my mom knew me too well and surprised me with it. She knew how much I loved sparkly things.

I carefully slipped on my dress, trying not to scratch myself from the sequins. I had to stop and admire myself in the mirror. The gold sequins caught the light and shimmered beautifully. The dress hugged my waist, showing off my small curves, and then flowed down into a form-fitting skirt. It was like it was made just for me. I could not wait to wear it out and show it off. To be honest, the dress might be a little too dressy for our dance. But that did not stop me from wearing it and twirling around in my room, pretending I was a movie star walking on the red carpet. I remembered trying on numerous dresses before finally settling on this one at the store. I knew it was the one as soon as I put it on. It made me feel confident and glamorous, like I could conquer the world.

"I found the . . . " My mother's voice trailed off. I turned around from my mirror, worried my zipper broke or I had something on the back of me.

"What is it, Mama?"

"You look so beautiful, Drea."

Smiling in appreciation, I turned back toward the mirror and said, "You think so?"

"Oh, yes. You look amazing. Let me take your picture." "Not in here, Mama. My room is a mess. Wait until I'm fully dressed and am wearing my shoes."

"Oh, here are the earrings. I found them in my bathroom of all places."

"Yes, thank you so much."

"Is Oliver meeting you here?"

""I'm not going with Oliver. I'm going with the girls and Daniel."

"Oh."

Her puzzled expression showed she wanted to ask more, but she didn't, so I said, "We already talked about it, and I'm meeting him there."

"Oh, okay." The phone rang.

"I'll get it. You finish getting dressed."

Twisting to my bed to anchor myself to put on my shoes, I heard Mama greeting Daniel.

My phone buzzed.

We're on our way, Harmony texted the group.

I quickly responded, Cool. Daniel is already here.

After a quick swipe of my Honest lip gloss and one more twirl in the mirror, I met Daniel in the living room.

Walking down the hallway, I saw Daniel first as he was playing on his phone.

"You beat the girls here."

He looked up, and his expression told me exactly how others would judge my outfit. He slid a grin on his face and only offered, "Wow."

"You don't look so bad yourself."

Daniel was dressed impeccably, with each detail put together to create a flawless look. His black pants hugged his legs perfectly, accentuating his tall and lean figure. The gold blazer he wore was a bold choice, outlined in sleek black material. The choice of black and gold was a testament to Daniel's classic taste.

"We look like the spring dance king and queen," he said, laughing.

"Yeah, except we aren't."

"You two look perfect," Mama said, standing by the door with her phone ready to take pictures.

The doorbell rang.

Mama opened the door, and Harmony and Noelle walked in, full of color and grace. Harmony chose to wear a stunning purple halter dress that highlighted her flawless figure. The halter neckline

drew the eye up and emphasized her toned arms while the deep purple hue complemented her complexion beautifully. What truly stood out was the way it showcased Harmony's assets. The fitted dress made her waist appear smaller and her hips and breast more noticeable.

Noelle projected the charm of a holiday Barbie in her black and gold puffy dress. The combination of these colors created a dramatic contrast that immediately captured attention. The dress's design added a touch of playfulness to her demeanor. The glistening black fabric swirled around Noelle's body, creating a sense of movement and fluidity. The sheen of the material added a touch of glamour, suitable for a holiday-themed Barbie.

The puffy sleeves not only added a charming touch to the dress but also gave it a festive feel. The gold accents on the sleeves elevated the dress to a whole new level. The skirt of the dress was like a tutu, with layers of tulle cascading down.

"Hello, Mrs. Ramsey," Harmony and Noelle said in unison before they headed straight to me.

"Girl, you look great," Harmony said, taking my hand and twirling me.

"You two look good. I love the purple on you, and I love the tutu dress."

"You know my mama made this?" Noelle asked, playing with the skirt.

"Really?" I said moving toward her to touch the dress to feel the material.

"Um, excuse me. I'm here too," Daniel said, adjusting the button on his jacket.

"Oh. Hey, Daniel," Noelle said, before turning her attention back to me.

"Alright. Y'all all get together so I can take some pictures," Mama said, directing us where to stand.

"Can you send it to Daddy and Auntie Jolie?"

"Yes, yes, yes. Now come on. Y'all get together now." "Mrs. Ramsey, can you send those pictures to me too? My granny would love to see everyone's outfits."

"Me too," Noelle chimed in while Daniel placed his phone in his pocket, obviously eager to go.

One photoshoot and a few airdrops later, we were piled into Mama's car. With Noelle's puffy dress monopolizing the middle of the back seat, I was grateful that we were only going down the street.

"God, I feel like a can of sardines."

"Oh, quit complaining, Noelle. We're less than a mile away from the school," I said, talking to her skirt because her head disappeared after we all squished into the backseat, leaving Daniel to enjoy the front seat.

"Alright, ladies and gentleman, you all can stop complaining because you're here," Mama said, pulling behind a car dropping off people as well. "Y'all walking back or am I picking y'all up.?"

"We'll probably walk back."

"Speak for yourself, Drea. I can't walk back to my house in these heels," Noelle said trying to scoot out of the car. "I barely made it to your house."

We spilled out of the car like a can of biscuits ready to be baked except we were ready to dance. "Whatever. Mama, I'll text you." "Okay, sweetie. Y'all have fun."

The anticipation grew as we made our way into the building. When we stepped inside, we were immediately met with a burst of color and life. There were trees, vines, and flowers adorned in every corner, filling the air with their sweet scents. It was as if we had stepped into a fairy tale. The walls were covered in murals of rolling hills and majestic waterfalls, transporting us to a different world altogether. Beautiful plastic butterflies fluttered around, adding to the enchanting atmosphere. And in the center of it all, a grand fountain stood, surrounded by statues of mythical creatures. We could not help but stand in awe at this breathtaking scenery.

"This must have cost a fortune," Harmony said, looking around in astonishment.

Daniel, also looking around, responded, "Well, we did have to pay fifty dollars to attend."

The school had truly outdone themselves with this transformation.

"Come on. Let's walk around," Noelle said, eager to show all the boys her new dress.

Spotting Oliver by the photo booth, I told the group, "I'll catch up with y'all later."

"You already ditching us for a man?" Daniel asked.

I gave him side eye because we both know he would do the same thing if he saw Christopher. But I only offered, "I won't be gone too long."

Disappearing in the crowd and reemerging on the other side of the gym by the photo booth, Oliver looked at me, and our eyes met. He looked so good walking toward me. He looked like an extra in one of those Mission Impossible movies. The black suit, coupled with the crisp white dress shirt underneath, made him look muscular.

"You look beautiful," he said, coming in for a kiss. The hunter green handkerchief neatly tucked into the jacket pocket sparkled as he kissed me softly on my lips.

"You clean up pretty well yourself." "You just got here?"

"Yeah, we just got dropped off." "Where is the rest of the dynamic trio?" "Oh, they are somewhere around here."

Taking a step back while I lifted up my arm, Oliver said, "Wow, Drea, you really look good. I need to show you off. Let's walk around."

His compliments made me blush. When he grabs my hand to hold, it sent a wave throughout my body. His hands were soft, and he did not squeeze my hand where my fingers were on top of each other. I loved this feeling, and I loved that he wanted to show me off.

As we made our way through the garden, we were greeted by our peers who were equally mesmerized. Everywhere we looked, there were students taking pictures, laughing, and simply basking in the beauty of this magical garden. The gymnasium had been divided into different sections, each representing a different season. From the vibrant colors of spring to the warm hues of autumn, it was a visual feast for the eyes. In each section, there were activities related to the season, allowing us to fully immerse ourselves in the experience.

"Hey, there's Harmony and Noelle. Why are they with Daniel?"

The lovey dove waves I was feeling in my back now turned into butterflies in my stomach.

Oliver asked again, "Drea, why is Daniel with your best friends?" When I saw the wrinkle appear on his forehead, my heart dropped. It was a bulging crease, a deep indentation that was almost scary to look at. It was a wrinkle of concern. And when he asked the question again, his voice was serious. It was clear that he already knew the answer, yet he needed confirmation from me.

My voice was shaky, and I didn't want to lose this moment, but I had to tell him the truth. "Daniel rode with us."

He let go of my hand and stepped back like he was trying to get another look at me. "Us as in he came to your house?"

What was once happy feelings of blushing now turned into uncomfortable feelings of guilt. "We all met at my house." "And you couldn't come with me? I'm your boyfriend." "Oliver, I know, but we had already planned on going together before you asked me to be your girlfriend."

His body language was becoming more and more distant from me. "You know how I feel about you two hanging out."

"And I told you we are just friends."

"So if I spent all my time with another girl and told you we were just friends, would you believe me?"

"First of all, we don't spend all of our time together. And secondly, I would believe you if you told me you two were just friends."

"I'm sorry. I'm not that naïve, and I don't believe you."

"Are you serious right now?" My guilt was quickly turning into anger. "You're doing this right now?" "If not now, then when, Drea?"

"You know what? I can't with you right now. I'll be back." "Where are you going?"

"To have fun with my friends!" I yelled back over the music.

I wanted him to feel my anger.

The sounds of music filled my ears, flowing down like a gentle waterfall. Each note transported me to a world of pure bliss, and I tried to melt all my worries and troubles away. There was a smile on my face and a spring in my step as I walked toward my friends, trying to be completely lost in the enchanting melodies. But as I walked closer to them, my excitement was disrupted by my conversation with Oliver and that smug look on his face. The mere thought of him was enough to bring me back to reality. I felt a surge of frustration and anger rise within me, threatening to ruin this beautiful moment. But I refused to let him taint my happiness. Not today. Not ever.

"Where is Oliver?" Daniel asked, looking around.

"He's over there somewhere," I said nonchalantly.

Harmony walked next to me, so she didn't have to yell over the music, and asked, "What happened, Drea?"

Just as I was about to answer, Beyonce's "Party" song came on. "Nothing, but I want to dance."

As someone who typically avoided drawing attention to myself, the idea of making a scene or dancing in public had always made me cringe. I had always been more comfortable blending into the background, observing and taking in my surroundings rather than becoming a part of it. But tonight was different. Maybe it was the new dress that fit me like a glove or the way the light hit my hair just right, but I felt like a million bucks. And for the first time in a long time, I didn't care what anyone else thought.

The beat pulsed through my body, giving me a sense of power and strength. With each step I took, I felt myself growing more confident and determined. It was not a planned or choreographed dance, but rather a spontaneous burst of energy and joy. I let myself be swept away by the music, and for once, I did not care who was watching. As I danced, I realized that I was finally not giving a fuck. I was not worried about looking silly or uncoordinated. I was not worried about what people might think of me. I was simply enjoying the moment and letting myself be free. To just be in the moment and not worry about anything else was a rare and wonderful feeling. And to my surprise, people were actually drawn to my energy because other girls, including my besties, met me on the dance floor. We were all singing the words to the song and each believing we were Beyonce.

Just as the second verse started, I saw Oliver walk over to Daniel. I was curious and anxious about what they were talking about, but I pretended to not care. I simply ignored him and continued dancing. He might have disrupted my peace for a moment, but I wouldn't let him ruin my night. I was looking too good and feeling too good to let anyone bring me down.

Unfortunately, as I was about to rap Andre 3000's verse, Noelle tugged on my arm and pointed at Oliver and Daniel. I shrugged my shoulders, trying not to worry. Daniel might not be able to check his parents, but he definitely did not have a problem checking his peers. Besides, maybe Oliver would believe Daniel when he told him we were only friends.

But Noelle's messy ass wanted to know what they were saying so she kept pressing the issue. "I think you should go over there to see what's going on."

"You mean you want to know what is going on."

"Yes, I mean, no." She sucked her teeth. "Girl, just come on."

The three of us left the dance floor and so did everyone else as the music changed to Marshmello's "Fell in Love." This would have been a cool song to dance with Oliver, but he would rather be angry and accuse me of going with Daniel.

"What's up?" I said, walking up on Daniel and Oliver. They looked like they were having a deep, philosophical conversation.

Daniel's hand was on his chin, and Oliver was using a lot of hand gestures like he was a mime.

"Nothing. Daniel and I were just talking."

Ignoring Oliver's statement because I still felt like he owed me an apology, I looked at Daniel for confirmation.

"Yeah, we cool. We're just talking. I was telling him why I came with y'all."

"Oh my God, Oliver. I've already told you this." "And I wanted to hear it from Daniel."

"So my word isn't good enough for you?"

"No, I didn't say that. I just wanted to talk to Daniel."

I was so annoyed at Oliver right now. Where was this jealous boyfriend act coming from? Where was the sweet guy I've known most of my life, the guy my dad liked? "Whatever, Oliver." I turned to Harmony and Noelle, who were listening intently to our disagreement. "Y'all want to get some punch?"

"No, not really," Noelle said.

I rolled my eyes at her because I knew that she wanted to say, "Hell, nah, and miss this juicy back and forth between Drea's lovers."

"Hey, I'll be back," Daniel said, breaking up the tense and uncomfortable moment.

I followed him with my eyes as he walked over to Christopher. They dapped up each other like two guys never bringing suspicion to themselves. They walked out of the gymnasium, and I was secretly happy that Daniel finally found someone he could be happy with too.

"Well, that was anticlimactic," Harmony blurted while checking her phone.

"Drea, can we talk?" Oliver asked, grabbing my hand.

I pulled my hand back and sternly said, "No. I want to enjoy the party."

Harmony and Noelle glanced at each other, not wanting to interfere but to continue to use my relationship mishap for their entertainment.

Looking surprised at my reaction to him, Oliver stormed away. His anger was radiating off him in waves. I could feel his fumes seeping toward me like a heavy fog as he disappeared into the crowd. It was as if his emotions were tangible, filling the space with an overwhelming weight. And even though I was not the one who caused this argument, I felt a little bit responsible.

"Come on, let's get something to drink," Noelle said, putting her arms around me.

With feelings of confusion and a hint of anger toward Oliver, I responded back, "Oh now you're thirsty?"

Chapter Twenty-Four

Present Day

I find myself back at Dr. E's office, thumbing through an Elle magazine with mama. Thoughts of the girls and my last interaction finds its way to the forefront of my mind. A lump in my throat settles as I am reminded that I don't know how to control my emotions. I am so scared I won't ever get better.

"Drea," Dr. E says with humor in her voice. I'm glad she can smile because laughter seems to escape me at the moment.

Walking back to her office, a heavy weight tugs at my heart. "Have a seat, Drea. Would y like anything to drink?"

"No, thanks."

"How are you feeling today?"

"Wait. You can't figure it out through my body language again?"

"I'm not a mind reader, Drea. Besides, what are you feeling right now?"

"I had an argument with my best friends, and I don't know how to fix it," I say, looking down in embarrassment.

"Was it over Daniel?" "Yeah, you can say that." "Why?"

I shrug my shoulders.

"Drea, do you trust me?" Dr. E's question is sincere and thoughtful.

"Yes, I think so."

"Then tell me what really happened to Daniel."

I pause. Talking about it in detail makes me uncomfortable, it's like it's happening all over again. Besides, what did that have anything to do with E and my argument with Noelle and Harmony?

Dr. E's eyes are piercing me as she waits on my response. I take a deep breath and exhale slowly.

I don't know where to start or what to say, so I blurt out, "Daniel came out to me, and I promised to take his secret to the grave, not even telling my other two best friends."

"Why?"

"Because I know Coral Bluff can be so judgmental, especially religious people. I didn't want Daniel to be an outcast like he was before moving here."

"So this happened before?"

"Yes, but not to this degree. His parents knew about it and made him go to this weekly church thing to pray out the gayness. His father was so mean and hard on him. I wish his mother would stand up to his father. But, anyway, it sounds ridiculous, but Daniel met Christopher there, at the church thing, and they fell for each other. So the night of our spring dance, Daniel left to talk to Christopher discreetly. Someone must have followed them and recorded the two of them kissing behind the school, and the video was leaked to every social media platform."

"Wow. That sounds problematic and very cruel for someone to do that to Daniel. Did they find the person or persons who did it?"

"No, people were more concerned with the video."

"And you think that was the reason Daniel took his life?" "I know it is. We spoke the day before. He had on a good face, trying to ignore the school's gossip, but I know he was hurting on the inside. But I assured him that the rumor mill would move on just like it did with the other rumors. I don't know what happened between the time we talked at school and the time he went home because he did it that night."

"And the video is what caused you and your other besties to fall out?"

"Partly. They felt like I should have told them about Daniel being gay, but I promised Daniel I would keep his secret."

"Drea."

"Yes?"

"Thank you for sharing that information with me. I know that was hard, but do you realize you were able to tell me the story of Daniel's suicide without crying or having a panic attack?"

I lean back in my chair and let out a deep breath, feeling a sense of relief come over me. It was a difficult conversation, one that I had been dreading for quite some time. But somehow, I managed to get through it without breaking down. It is funny how certain moments can have such a significant impact on us. This conversation was not any ordinary exchange of words; it was a defining moment for me. A moment where I had to confront my deepest fears and insecurities.

"I think because you're easy to talk to."

"Perhaps. Or maybe you're going through the process of fully grieving and accepting. Drea, you're stronger than you think."

"Sometimes I don't feel strong. I mean, I break down so easily."

"Correction. You used to break down so easily. I haven't handed you a tissue since we started this session."

As I sit here, rubbing my hands across the comforting velvet of the sofa, I reflect on the last three days. These last few days has obviously been restorative for my mental health, but I ask myself, Am I strong? I am still struggling to receive Dr. E's answer. But she is right; I have not had another panic attack, and I am freely talking about Daniel.

"Dr. E, can I ask you a question?" "Of course. Go for it."

"Next Monday, the school is having a memorial for Daniel.

Do you think I'm strong enough to attend?"

"I don't see why not. You sat across from me and told a complete stranger your most vulnerable moments. You don't think you can be present among people you know?"

"Yeah, but I feel like it's easy talking to you. You're not judgy. Kids can be cruel. I've been cruel to people before so I know."

"What are you most afraid of if you attend next Monday?"

"It may trigger me if I hear anyone try to slander his name because he was gay. He wanted to live in his truth as a gay teen, but that is what also led to him kill himself. I don't think I'm strong enough to hear any type of jokes or anything about him."

To my surprise, Dr. E. does not react immediately. She is known for her quick thinking and ability to respond to any situation with the right words to say. But this time was different. She leans back in her chair and starts chewing on the tip of her signature candy cane pen. I cannot help but feel a bit unsettled. Did I say something wrong? Did she not know how to respond? My mind is racing with questions and insecurities. I try to interpret her actions.

And then Dr. E finally speaks, "I'm sorry. I needed a moment to process what you said. Let me start by saying that I believe sexuality is a spectrum, and everyone falls somewhere on that spectrum. It is not a simple matter of being either straight or gay.

There are many shades in between, and it is possible for someone's sexuality to change and evolve over time. Sexuality is complex, and there is no one-size-fits-all definition. It is entirely possible that Daniel could have been suppressing his true feelings for years, and now he was ready to embrace his true self. Or maybe he has always known but was too afraid to come out due to societal pressures and fear of judgement."

She let out a deep exhale and continued, "However, there are still many people who face discrimination and prejudice for their sexual orientation. This can create a fear of coming out and being open about who they truly are. The fact that we are even discussing Daniel's sexuality shows there is a stigma attached to being gay.

Many people from the LGBTQ+ community often struggle with being open about their sexuality, partly due to society's expectations and misconceptions. You are a great friend, Drea, and as much as this situation hurts, maybe part of the healing is educating."

"Educating? Who and what can I teach?"

"Love and compassion. Even if people never accept the fact he identified as gay, you can teach people to have compassion for everyone, despite our differences."

"And how can I do that? This is a memorial for Daniel. I don't even know if I'm able to attend without breaking down."

"You show people through the friendship you two shared. You never judged him. In fact, you kept his secret close to your chest. That's a hard thing to do, especially at your age."

"But I need more than to show our friendship. How can I show people who Daniel really was?

"Now that is something only Drea can answer, and believe me, you have the answer."

Her response does not put me at ease. In fact, it confuses me even more. And just when I thought I had all of this shit figured out, I am back at square one.

CHAPTER TWENTY-FIVE

APRIL 2023

Sunday came around, inviting me to wake up, but I refused to get out of bed. I lay in bed, thinking about last night. Instead of daydreaming of flirting and dancing with Oliver, I thought about the argument we had. I had not seen or spoken to Oliver since he stormed off. Daniel also had yet to respond to my texts. This whole mess started when tensions were running high between Oliver and me. I wished Oliver were not jealous of Daniel and my friendship. I wished I could tell him the truth and make him comfortable with my friendship with Daniel. But I couldn't.

However, I was proud of myself for not overthinking and shutting down. I had a great time with my girls. And for a moment, I forgot all about Oliver's absence. But as the night came to an end and it was time to head home, I realized that Daniel was still missing. While he had assured me that he could find his own way home, I could not help but worry. I tried texting Daniel multiple times last night, but my messages went unanswered. And now, as I lay here on this lazy Sunday morning, my mind was consumed with thoughts of what could have happened. Did Oliver and Daniel have

another fight? Did something happen to Daniel on his way home?

I rolled back over on my side and noticed a burst of color.

Flowers swaying gently in the soft breeze and starting to bloom right outside my window were more clues that spring was here. There were rows of pink tulips Mama planted last year, hoping they would bloom. Their delicate petals were gently dancing in the wind.

Just as I finally made up my mind to get out of the bed and use the toilet, Harmony called me on FaceTime.

"Hey, Harmony."

"How can you still be in the bed?" "It's only nine-thirty."

"You must haven't been on Snapchat or IG." "No. I literally just woke up. Why?"

"Hold on. I'm sending it to you right now." "Sending me what?"

"Just check your messages."

I clicked on Harmony's message out of pure curiosity, and little did I know what I was about to witness. I sat there, paralyzed, as my heart sank deeper and deeper into my stomach. It was one of the most unsettling videos I had ever seen. As the video continued, I felt a sense of helplessness and anger coming over me, and I could not do anything but watch in horror. The more I watched, the more nauseous I felt. The images were etching themselves into my mind, and it was almost too much to handle. My body involuntarily tensed up. My hands shook as I clenched my right hand into a fist. I could not believe someone would record Daniel and Christopher kissing, two people sharing a private moment, and upload it to social media "Harmony, I gotta call you back."

I jumped out of bed and washed up before I threw on some clothes. I needed to see Daniel. Since he was not answering my texts, I would not bother calling him. I would just walk over to his house.

My phone was going off from numerous notifications. I could only assume it was from what I just watched.

As I made my way to Daniel's house, I could feel my heart pounding against my chest with every step. My emotions were in disarray, and my nerves were frayed. The anticipation of what lay ahead made my heart race and my mind race even faster. But throughout the chaos, I was lost in my thoughts, wondering what I would say to him. As my foot connected with the pavement, I could feel my heart trying to escape my chest. It was as if my heart were trying to physically manifest the emotional turmoil within me. The faster I walked, the more pronounced this feeling became. Despite the overwhelming internal chaos, I continued to move forward. If anything, the intensity of my emotions only served as a reminder of how much I cared for Daniel. He became one of my best friends.

And I knew how closed-minded this town could be. With that video out, who knew what he was going through? And what were his parents thinking?

As I approached his house, I felt knots in my stomach. My heart was beating so fast that I could barely catch my breath. I took a deep breath and rang the doorbell. Seconds seemed like hours as I waited for Daniel to open the door. Maybe they all went to church? But, surprisingly, I was met by his father.

Swallowing a thick blob of spit and with my hands shaking, I spoke, "Hello, Mr. Gardner. Is Daniel home?"

The silence was deafening as he stood in front of me, his arms folded, and his expression detached. I could feel a chill run down my spine as I tried to meet his gaze, but I found myself unable to look directly at him. His mere presence was intimidating, and the fact that he has not said a word only added to my growing fear. I shifted my weight from one foot to the other, trying to break the tense silence that had settled between us. But he remained unmoving. I felt like a caged animal, trapped and helpless under his intense stare.

I began to wonder if I had done something to provoke this reaction from him. Did I offend him in some way? Did he think I posted the video? My mind raced with possibilities, each one more terrifying than the last. The longer he remained silent, the more my anxiety grew. But then, just as I was about to give in to my fear and run away, he spoke, "Daniel is not available." His deep, authoritative voice broke through the silence, and I felt my heart skip a beat. His words were few, but they were powerful.

"I just wanted to check on him." I couldn't believe I was somewhat pushing back against his father. Daniel did not even go against his father.

"He's unavailable to talk," he said again, but with more directness in his voice.

Mr. Gardner was not yielding, and I did not know if Daniel had his phone to respond back to my texts messages.

But I had to push one more time. "Can you tell him I stopped by?"

But without another word, Mr. Gardener stepped back into his house and closed the door in my face. I stood on the porch a few seconds in shock and disbelief. Feeling frustrated and a little embarrassed, I walked back home, trying to make sense of what had just happened.

By the time I got home and checked my phone, I had over eighty notifications and text messages from social media, Harmony, Noelle, and Oliver.

Drea, we need to come over. Where are you?

Why aren't you responding back?

The texts messages from our group chat continued until I finally replied, I'm home. Y'all can come over.

I did not really feel like being bothered or like I was getting the third degree. But I also did not want to be by myself when my thoughts got like this.

We are on our way, Noelle responded.

Harmony and Noelle must have been on their way to my house because they arrived within a couple of minutes of Noelle's text.

I could not get through the door good when Noelle came in ready to be messy. "Girl, I know you've seen that video from last night."

Now, any other time, I would love some juicy gossip, but not when it involved one of my close friends; it did not feel good.

"Yeah. Harmony sent it to me."

"And . . . ?"

"And what, Noelle? I didn't post it. I mean, how do we know if it's even real? It could be some AI video."

Harmony was still standing by the front door when her eyebrows flew up from my speculation. "AI? Are you crazy? That was not an AI video. That was Daniel and Christopher Evans kissing, and it was passionate too. Wait, Noelle, didn't you use to talk to Christopher?"

"Briefly. We just didn't hit it off, and I thought it was me.

Now I know he's just not into girls." Harmony and Noelle both laughed.

"Y'all think this is funny? Two people's reputations are ruined because of this video."

"Wait." Harmony walked over to me. "Did you know Daniel was gay?"

"What? No, of course not. We never talked about his sexuality nor was it my business."

"But you were in love with him, and then y'all became friends. It doesn't make sense."

"It doesn't have to make sense to you, Harmony. And I wasn't in love with him. I really liked him, and after working on our project together, we became closer and decided we were better off as friends." I felt my bottom lip tremble because I hated lying, especially to my best friends, but I also promised Daniel I would never tell his secret. I hated that someone else did.

They both stood in my living room, Noelle wanting more gossip and Harmony wanting the truth. Harmony was not buying my story, and I understood why. Her suspicion was warranted. After all, my actions and words did not exactly align, making me appear more guilty than innocent. But I did not attempt to convince her otherwise. Why? Because trying to prove my innocence would only make me look more conniving.

So I changed the subject. "And why are we only focusing on Daniel and Christopher? There is someone going around filming private moments. Who's to say another video of us in the locker room won't get out? We need to find out who recorded and posted this."

"And how would we do that?" Noelle asked.

"I don't know. I guess we can start with the technology club at school."

"I'm not about to be on some witch hunt with you. I have two priorities: school and my son."

"Well, sign me up. I'm all for a good story."

Harmony rolled her eyes at Noelle's comment and continued, "Why are you dressed? You don't get out of bed this early on Sundays."

"I walked over to Daniel's house to check on him."

Noelle's ears perked back up. "And?"

"His daddy said he was unavailable."

"So you walked all the way over to Daniel's house to check on him?"

"Yeah. Why?"

"Have you even spoken to Oliver? Remember him? Your boyfriend?"

Harmony was right. I got so consumed with the video, I forgot about Oliver and us not speaking after last night's fight.

"I take that as a no."

"Harmony, what's your problem with Daniel?"

"Nothing. I just think it's strange you become besties with this transfer student no one knows nothing about. Your boyfriend doesn't like him.

And now a video of him kissing one of our football starters doesn't make sense. And what really doesn't make sense is you saying you didn't know any of it."

"I don't know what you want me to say." "The truth."

Noelle's gaze was going back and forth between Harmony and me like she was watching a tennis match and I was losing.

Noelle had to save me. "Okay, okay, okay. Will you two calm down? Harmony, won't your granny and Matthew be back from church soon?"

Harmony was looking at me but responded, "Yeah." "We should get going. Drea, we'll see you tomorrow morning."

"I might not walk with y'all tomorrow."

"Harmony, why not?" Noelle asked. "I don't want to be seen with a liar."

I rolled my eyes and folded my arms, giving her the "whatever" demeanor.

"Alright, let's go. Y'all both in y'all feelings." "Bye."

And just like that, my world was once again flipped upside down.

CHAPTER TWENTY-SIX

It was Monday morning, and I was dreading going to school.

I could feel the anxiety building up in my stomach as I thought about all the gossip that would inevitably surround me. When the video was put up, the speculation started pouring in. People were quick to jump to conclusions and question if Daniel and Christopher were actually a couple or if the video were fake news. Some even accused Daniel of seducing Christopher for his own fame and popularity. The comments and discussions seemed never-ending, and it was hard not to get caught up in it all. I could only imagine what the next eight hours at school would bring.

Before I left the house, I checked my phone to see if Daniel responded to my thirty-something messages and five missed calls, but he did not. I felt like he was avoiding me like the plague, and I could not blame him. After all, the whole school was talking about him, and he probably did not want to face the judgment and ridicule. I felt sick to my stomach as I thought about going to school and facing everyone's stares and whispers. Would they see me as a naive friend who did not know what was going on right under her nose?

Would they think I was a fool for not seeing the signs? I knew deep down that it was not my fault and that I should not be ashamed or embarrassed. But in high school, rumors were like a virus that spread quickly and infected everyone in its path. I did not want to be a part of it. I did not want to be the topic of discussion for something that had nothing to do with me. And yet, as much as I wanted to stay home and avoid it all, I could not. I had to face the music and go to school. Besides, I would not let him go through the snide comments and stares alone.

I do not think I have ever gotten to school as fast as I did today. Each step felt urgent as I weaved my way through the students milling about.

I scanned the crowd, looking for Daniel's familiar face. Suddenly, I saw him walking toward me with a heavy- looking backpack slung over his shoulder. And as soon as Daniel appeared, the whispering and snickering started again. It seemed as though the mere sight of him was enough to trigger a wave of mockery from those around him. People whispered, pointed, and laughed while someone even had the audacity to yell out "Where's your boyfriend?" But despite the cruel words and gestures, Daniel kept his head high and walked with dignity, not giving any evidence of embarrassment.

I could not speak; all I knew to do was go up and hug him, and that is what I did. We stood by our lockers, hugging for what seemed like minutes. He hugged me back like he wanted to transfer some of the weight of embarrassment onto me so he could take a break.

"Thank you, Drea," Daniel said with tears in his eyes.

My heart skipped a beat as I took in his disheveled appearance and tired eyes, but I quickly composed myself and put on a reassuring smile. I noticed the dark circles under his eyes and his tired expression.

"You don't have to thank me. I'm your friend. How are you holding up?"

"As best as expected."

"You gotta keep your head up high and not let these judgmental dummies think they won."

"I don't know, Drea. I just need a break from it all. I'm getting it from my parents, the neighbors, the church, and now school. I don't know how much more I can take."

"Are your parents really mad?"

"My father practically disowned me. He hasn't really spoken to me since the video came out. I heard him tell my mother that we probably need to move again. Drea, I'm so tired of running and feeling like I can't be myself. When will all this end?"

I wished I could make everything better for him, but I knew that was not possible. "I don't know, Daniel, but you can't give up. Just can't."

He tried to form a smile on his face, but I knew he was hurting inside.

"Hey, you want to come over after school? We can just hang out and laugh like we used to."

"Thanks for the offer, but I can't. My mother is scared for my safety and is picking me up after school."

"Seriously? Has it gotten that bad?"

"This morning, I heard my dad tell my mother that he received a few spam calls. And our neighbors have distanced themselves, not even making eye contact with any of us. You would think I killed someone. All I did was kiss a boy. A boy who I really, really liked." I could see tears starting to form back into his eyes. "It's not fair, Drea."

I pulled him close and hugged him again. "It's going to be okay, Daniel. I promise."

"How do you know?"

"Because nothing lasts forever, not even gossip. Watch. You'll see. Everyone will be talking about something different by next week."

"You think so?"

"I know so. People's attention span is so short they will move on to the next big thing that catches their attention."

"Thank you for being here for me. And I know you came by yesterday. My dad was so furious; I was surprised he opened the door for you."

"It's whatever. I just wanted to check on you once I heard. Have you talked to Christopher?"

"I think that's what hurts the most. No, I haven't heard from him since the video was released. We shared a special moment that night, and now he has blocked me on everything. Have you seen him?"

"No, I haven't seen him."

"Why does this keep happening to me?"

"What?"

"Every time I start to like someone, it always ends up falling apart. When will it be my turn to be happy?"

"I told you once we graduate and leave this backwards-ass town."

"Yeah, I remembered. I must wait two more years?"

I did not say anything. I did not know how to sell the idea that two years would fly by and we would be so happy in another city. I could not say that because I did not know for sure if that would happen.

"Come on. Let's get to class before we are late. You don't have to worry about anything."

"I love your optimism, Drea, but people are talking now and will continue to talk."

Daniel was right. As the day went on, the teasing and mean comments continued, but Daniel tried to look like he was unbothered. He went about his day as if nothing was out of the ordinary. But it was evident that his resilience was wearing him down and the bullies' comments were starting to get under his skin.

"Do you have a purse to match those tight ass pants you're wearing?" a senior said as we passed him in the hallway. Everyone within ear shot started laughing.

"Just ignore his stupid ass," I said trying to reassure Daniel, but I felt him pulling away.

The last period of the day could not come soon enough.

Daniel and I sat next to each other, listening to Mrs. Dixon go over the consequences of industrialization. My mind wandered off, and I realized I had not seen or spoken to Oliver or the girls today. In fact, Ms. Paisley had not said one word to Daniel or me. I did not think she even looked our way during our classes. I had been so focused on making sure Daniel was comfortable, I forgot about everyone else.

The sound of the bell scared me back to reality, and I heard Mrs. Dixon assigning homework.

"What did she say?" I asked Daniel as we both pack up our book bags and walked toward the front entrance.

"We have to finish reading chapter twelve and answer the knowledge questions at the end of the chapter."

"Got it. So you're going straight home, huh?" "Yeah. And you know what's wild?"

"What?"

"I hate being at home, but I would rather be there than to be here at school."

"I can see that. I mean, these kids are so rude and stupid." "It just feels good being by myself in my room with my thoughts. At least there I'm not being judged or made fun of." "Well, you're not alone. You got me."

"Thanks, Drea, for always being a good friend to me even when I was being a shitty friend to you."

Daniel scooped me up in his arms. A wave of overwhelming anxiousness flooded me. It was not just any hug; it felt different from the hug this morning. t almost felt like a goodbye hug. The way he held on to me, his grip tight and his body pressed against mine, almost felt like he was trying to hold on to something that was slipping away. Our friendship was strong, unbreakable, despite what was going on. So why did this hug feel so final?

I pulled away from Daniel's embrace and looked up at him, searching for any signs of what was going on in his mind. But all I saw was a blank expression, masking the turmoil that I knew was going on inside. "Are you going to be okay?"

"Yeah, I"ll be fine. I'll talk to you later."

"I'll text you tonight," I said as he turned away and walked out of the front door. He looked down as he briskly walked toward his mother's car, trying to avoid the stares and more rude comments.

I felt a little uneasy about Daniel's mental state, but I knew once he got through this mess, he would be able to get through anything. That reassurance made me feel good, and I put my bookbag on both of my shoulders and walked out the front door with my head raised high.

Going back home, my memory took me back to this morning. I was feeling down and defeated, unsure of what the day would bring. I felt overwhelmed and stressed about how Daniel would handle the gossip and act toward me. But as I made my way back home at the end of the day, I noticed a significant shift in my emotions. Now, instead of feeling glum, I felt hopeful and optimistic. It was amazing how much a single day can change things. But now, as I reflected on my day, I realized that none of those worries seemed quite as impossible as I initially thought.

People were so fickle, they just gravitated to the latest gossip. But I was no stranger to gossip. Last school year, the biggest school gossip was Harmony's pregnancy. The school went up in an uproar because no one could have seen that coming, especially with the douchebag she was dating. Luckily for Harmony, her grandmother made her do ninth grade remote so when she came back this year it was like everyone forgot she even had baby Matthew.

Life could be so unpredictable. Just like how my mood had transformed throughout the day, life could take unexpected turns in a matter of moments.

When I reached my porch, the buzzing in my pocket alerted me that I had either a text message or a notification. Walking in, my nose scanned the house to see if could smell any familiar scents of food since Mama was home when I left this morning. But my nose did not pick up anything. Which meant I'll be eating leftovers or ordering from DoorDash.

A little disappointed, I reached for my phone and prepared to search for food when I saw a text message from Oliver.

Did you miss me at school?

I barely thought about him. But I responded, I did miss you.

Why didn't you come to school?

I'm sick.

Is it COVID?

Nah, just allergies.. 'Do you need anything? Nope.

I'll hit you up later to check on you.

He hearted my message. I exhaled as I got out of being accused of not being thoughtful. Being a good girlfriend was stressful. I did not know how Harmony and Noelle did it.

That reminded me that I did not see the girls today either. I texted our group, Hey, I didn't see y'all today. Y'all good?

Noelle typed back first. I was around. I was working on my final project in the library for Mr. Brown's class.

I thumbs-upped her message.

Harmony did not respond back. I did not know if she were still mad at me or if she were busy with her baby. Either way, I still felt a little uneasy about how we got off track. I knew we would move on from it. We always did, but only time would tell when.

Chapter Twenty-Seven

Tuesday morning hit me like a ton of bricks. Yesterday was rough, and I just couldn't wait for all this mess to blow over.

Walking to school by myself wasn't so fun either. Everything had changed, and deep down, I knew that nothing would I ever go back to being the same as it was. Daniel's life had been turned inside out, and I didn't know where Oliver and I would go in our relationship. Plus, my besties and I had been in a weird space lately. I guessed Harmony was more upset than she admitted, and Noelle did not want to be in the middle of our mess. But I must admit, I had started to feel a little out of the loop. Our usual group chat had been eerily silent, and my text messages had gone unanswered.

As time went by with little to no responses, I felt a little hurt. I knew it was not a big deal in the grand scheme of things. It was a few missed messages, right? But it was hard not to take it personally when my best friends did not seem interested in talking to me.

Especially when I was used to being in constant communication. It was a scary to think that something so small that did not even involve them could potentially ruin our friendship.

Walking into school seemed terrifying. What would people say today about Daniel? About me? I headed straight to my locker and then to homeroom to wait for Daniel.

"Hey, Drea. What up?"

I turned around to see Oliver making his way through the crowd of students.

I bit my bottom lip as I was not ready to face him or anyone who was mad at me. "Hey, Oliver," I said, looking down at my Air Force Ones, too embarrassed to look him in the eyes.

"Can I walk you to your first period?" he asked, lifting my chin up with his index finger.

"Sure. I see you're feeling better today."

"Yeah, I couldn't stay home with my mother another day." "Why? Was it that bad?"

"No, not really. She just treats me like a baby whenever I get sick. It's almost annoying."

"Oh, is that all? That's your mother being a mother," I said, feeling awkward.

I felt people's eyes on me. My heart started to race, and my hands were becoming disgustingly sweaty.

Oliver grabbed my hand and said, "It's okay, Drea. I'm right here with you." He must have noticed my uncomfortable look as I kept my head down.

"I just want to get my books out of my locker and get to class. This day cannot go by fast enough."

"That video did some damage."

"Ugh, don't remind me," I said, reaching into my locker and using it as a shield to protect me from the onlookers.

"Listen. I want to talk to you about Saturday night."

Uh-oh, and here it goes. I swallowed my spit and turned toward him. "Look, Oliver. I'm sorry I didn't tell you Daniel was riding with us. I knew if I told you, you would get mad, and you did."

He placed my books down in my locker and took both of my hands into his hands and said, "Drea, I want to apologize to you. My behavior was immature, and I messed up both of our nights."

I jerked my head back. I couldn't believe Oliver came to his senses and apologized to me. "Thank you. That means a lot to me."

"I mean, you two are clearly friends." "What does that supposed to mean?"

"Oh, come on, Drea. I know you've seen the video of Daniel and Christopher. He's definitely not into girls," he said before laughing.

"How do you know if that video is even real? It could be AI generated."

"Really? You believe that?"

"I don't know, but I do know I wasn't there to see if it did or didn't happen."

"Well, someone was, and now it's everywhere."

"Oliver, two people's reputations are ruined over that stupid video. Don't you understand? Whether that video is real or not, Daniel is my friend, and his reputation is ruined."

Looking deep into my eyes, Oliver's face went from amused to empathetic. "I'm sorry, Drea. You're right."

"Thank you for apologizing. I wish other people would be as open and empathetic toward him as you."

He leaned in to kiss me, and his lips felt comforting like a hug. His kiss eased away some of the tension that was building up in my stomach. I kept my eyes closed after we stopped kissing because I did not want to leave that brief moment of serenity.

"You're such a good kisser, Drea."

"So are you."

"Let me walk you to class now so I won't be late for mine.

You want to meet up after school? I can walk you home." "Sure."

"Drea?"

"Yeah."

"I'm not only your boyfriend, but I want to be your best

friend too. You don't have to feel like you can't tell me anything."

He kissed me on the cheek as he walked away and left me standing in the doorway of my first period class.

By the time I came down from cloud one thousand, I scanned the room and noticed Daniel was not there. I walked in and heard whispers and snickering.

"Where is your best girlfriend?" Paisley asked, and the entire class erupted in laughter.

I was furious. This was the same person who literally threw herself at Daniel's feet and was butthurt when he rejected her.

"It must be exhausting to constantly try and bring others down just to make yourself feel better. Is that one of your coping mechanisms since Daniel rejected you so many times?"

The class sound like a choir when they said, "OOOHHH."

Paisley looked taken aback. She was used to being praised and admired for her looks and mean words, but this time, my words hit her hard. She took a deep breath and looked at me with vengeful eyes, but I rolled my eyes and walked to my seat. I sat next to the empty seat my best friend Daniel would occupy once he came.

It was a small win, but it felt good. I only wished Daniel could be here to see that he did not have to be scared of facing people. We could face these people together.

But as the day went on, the gossip only intensified. People were taking sides, making assumptions, and spreading false information just for the sake of getting attention. It was frustrating to see how easily people believed everything they saw on social media without knowing the full story. This experience was making me realize the power of social media. It could shape opinions, manipulate perceptions, and create false narratives. But most importantly, it showed me how easily we could get caught up in the mess of Daniel and Christopher kissing instead of seeing the truth of two human beings in love.

When I reached Mr. Fitzgerald's science class, I checked my phone to see if Daniel or the girls had texted me. Nobody reached out to me, and that unsettling feeling of disappointment rushed over me. My thoughts raced from one assumption to the next. Was Daniel avoiding school because his parents were trying to stay ahead of the scandal? Did Harmony feel betrayed because I kept Daniel's sexuality a secret? Why was Daniel's sexuality a topic of conversation anyway?

I tried to shake off the thoughts and sat next to Daniel's empty chair. I smiled to myself as my memories took me back to first semester when Daniel and I became partners for our science project. We had definitely had a bumpy friendship.

Doodling and daydreaming filled the remaining part of my day until the dismissal bell rang. I quickly collected my belongings and walked to my locker where I saw Oliver leaning against it.

"Hey, you," I said, poking him in the back.

"Hey," he said, returning my poke with a kiss on the cheek. "You want to stop by Burger Palace and get something to eat?"

"Nah. I have to finish my paper for English that's due tomorrow." And I wanted to see if I could get in touch with Daniel,

but I kept that part to myself.

"Oh, okay. I guess I can go to my worksite a little earlier than when I leave your place."

"How often do you work there?"

"Four days out the week for about two to three hours a day. Nothing too long because my mom doesn't want me falling behind in my grades."

"It must be nice to have both of your parents in the house checking in on you."

"I don't know. I guess it's cool until I do something wrong and they both gang up on me. That part sucks."

"Yeah, but it's worth it."

Neither one of us responded. I think we were both thinking of what to say next, and Oliver won.

"Do you wish your parents were still together? Is that why you said that?"

His question felt like someone sucker punched me in the stomach. The wind left my body as I was reminded of the feelings I experienced when my parents divorced two years ago. Oliver's question might seem like a simple and straightforward question, but for me, it brought up a surge of emotions and memories that I had long suppressed. No one had ever asked me that before, not even my parents.

After their divorce, my father moved out, and my mother returned to work full time. They went on with their lives as if the divorce never happened, leaving Franklin and me to figure things out on our own. Somehow, I felt a responsibility to take care of the house and bury the pain and confusion that I was feeling. I tried to put on a brave face for my friends, but I could not help but wonder why my family had fallen apart.

"Um, yeah. Yeah, I do wish my parents were still together. We shared a bond, a special bond, that worked. Now my dad is six hundred miles away, and I barely see my mom because of her work schedule. It's a little busy, but I make it work."

"Sometimes adults can be hard to talk to, but I do believe your parents are proud of you. Even if they don't tell you all the time."

"Thank you, Oliver. That was sweet to say."

I hugged him and placed my books in my locker before we walked home. His words filled up my heart, and although my family life was not my ideal situation, I really did know my parents loved me.

"Thank you for walking me home."

"No problem. I want to spend time with you."

I could feel my face turning hot as I was blushing. I leaned in to kiss him, this time making the first move. He slowly wrapped both of his hands around my waist, pulling me close to him. I feel his tongue slip into my mouth, and I reciprocated with my tongue.

This dance seemed to go on for some time until I felt a sensation in my pants. My eyes shot open, and I quickly stepped back, fearing that I may have peed my pants.

"What's wrong?"

"Nothing, I have to use the bathroom. Plus, I don't want you to be late for your job."

Looking confused but not objecting, he said, "Uh, okay. I'll text you later."

"Okay. Bye."

I ran up the porch and maneuvered my keys into the door.

Once I got on the other side of the front door, I let out a big exhale. I placed my bookbag on the floor and ran to the bathroom. Trying to unbutton my skinny, black, Express jeans, I felt embarrassed.

I hope I didn't pee on myself.

When I slid down my pants and panties, I plopped on the toilet confused as to why the sensation of having to pee quickly vanished. And after I further examined my panties and saw a clear wet stain in the seat part, I realized that I did not pee my pants but got excited by my boyfriend.

The first person I wanted to tell was Harmony, but I had not spoken or seen her since Sunday. So I extended the first olive branch and texted her apart from our group thread.

Hey. I'm sorry.

I knew those words might not be enough, but I truly meant them. I did not know what else to say at that moment. I hoped she could understand and forgive me. I knew apologies could feel empty and meaningless, especially when the damage had been done. But we had been friends forever and had been through worst.

I sat in the bathroom with my thoughts swirling around me like a storm. I closed my eyes and took a deep breath, focusing on the feeling of forgiveness that was slowly taking over me.

CHAPTER TWENTY-EIGHT

Walking into the homeroom, I was the second student to arrive, which was very rare. Daniel and I usually arrived right before the late bells rang. Going to my seat, I felt the sleep monster creeping up as I had another restless night except it was from the excitement Oliver left me. But I knew once Daniel arrived, I would be in a much better mood. He just had that type of effect on me.

Everyone was in their seats before the last bell rang.

Everyone except for Daniel. I glanced at my phone, but there were no text messages from him.

"Alright, class, let me check attendance before you all start talking," Mrs. Holmer said.

Daniel had not arrived yet, but I was not nervous. He could be running late or maybe he decided not to come to school today. I was not nervous yet. But to be on the safe side, I discreetly texted him. Hey, you're good?

I quickly placed my phone in my back pocket before Mrs. Holmer saw me. I would also be able to feel it vibrate once Daniel texted back.

First period was a blur as I tried my best to focus on the lesson, but my mind kept wandering back to the unanswered text message I had sent to Daniel. Lunchtime came and went with no sign of Daniel. I could feel my mood starting to take a nosedive as I wondered if Daniel were okay. By the afternoon, I did not know if my sleepiness was weighing on me or the fact I had not heard from Daniel. Either way I was getting nervous.

When I reached Mr. Fitzgerald's class, I was exhausted. My lack of sleep was starting to take its toll as I struggled to stay awake and focused. The exhaustion was making me irritable, and I did not want to snap on my classmates, so I kept to myself. I sat at the back table Daniel and I usually took when we want to pass notes to each other without getting caught.

I doodled on my notebook, not paying attention to today's lesson. I glanced at the clock and felt some reassurance as I only had one more class that stood between me and my bed. Getting back to my work of art on my notebook, there was a light knock on Mr. Fitzgerald's door.

Ms. Kahn, one of our school's counselors, walked in. But there was something different about her today. She usually had a bubbly demeanor, but right now it was replaced with a look of concern. She was dressed in a brown and burgundy suit, paired with nude shoes. Her haircut usually added a touch of sophistication to her appearance, but today, it made her look older than her age. Her face appeared wider, and her eyes were glassy.

"Mr. Fitzgerald, may I speak to you outside for a moment?"

I put down my pen and directed my attention to the two adults outside the classroom. I saw Ms. Kahn talking and Mr. Fitzgerald grabbing his mouth like he was trying to keep himself from vomiting. His face turned from shock to grief in a matter of seconds. As I was trying to figure out what the hell happened, I instantly wished Daniel were here. We always make up commentary for people when we people-watch, especially during class when we passed notes to each other. It was fun, and he was missing this. I wondered what storyline he would give to Mr. Fitzgerald and Ms. Kahn. Maybe they were secretly dating, and she was breaking it off with him. Whatever it was, I wanted to know.

They both finally returned to the class. Ms. Kahn was a petite woman and a soft voice. But today, she seemed focused and determined as she made her way to the front of the classroom.

Mr. Fitzgerald spoke first. "Hey, listen up, everyone. Ms. Kahn has some very important news to share with you."

Her usually calm and soothing voice had a sense of urgency to it. "Students, I don't quite know how to say this." She focused her eyes toward me. "One of your classmates committed suicide last night."

Everyone was taken back. Some people started whispering; another person let out a big gasp. I did not know how to process what she was saying. I saw her lips moving, but I was looking around the room, trying to figure out who committed suicide.

She continued talking, and her voice returned to my ears. "Daniel was a great student and had some close friends here. I know this may be a difficult time for everyone one, but please remember our office is open if you ever want to talk."

Wait. What? Daniel. Daniel committed suicide?!

****

Daniel is dead? It was the only thing that was left dangling in my ear. I suddenly felt my chest tighten. It was like someone had put a rope around my lungs, making it impossible for me to breathe. Panic set in as I frantically gasped for air, my mind racing with fear and confusion. I knew I had to get out of there. Without thinking, I dropped my book bag and phone and ran out of the classroom. I did not care about the confused looks I received from my classmates. I heard Ms. Kahn and Mr. Fitzgerald call my name, but I did not stop. I could not stop. I would literally die if I did not get any fresh air.

All I could think about was getting some air into my lungs.

I ran as fast as I could through the hallways until I reached the front entrance. I burst out of the school building and into the crisp, fresh air. I collapsed onto the ground, gasping for breath. It felt like my body was betraying me, making it nearly impossible for me to intake the air that I so desperately needed. It was a terrifying feeling, one that I had never experienced before. I felt tears falling down my face as I tried to regulate my breathing. The world around me suddenly disappeared. The sounds of chatter and footsteps faded into the background as my vision blurred and darkness surrounded me. What was happening? I tried to focus, but my mind was clouded, and my body felt heavy. What was going on? And then nothing. I blacked out or lost consciousness. The next thing I remembered was waking up in the nurse's office with my mother and Auntie Jolie standing over me.

"Oh, thank God she's awake. Drea, are you okay, baby?" Mama was hugging me so tightly I could barely respond to her question.

"What happened?" I could see the worry in their eyes, and it made me realize that something serious had happened. I felt a surge of fear and confusion.

"You had a panic attack and fainted, Drea. But you're okay now," the nurse said as she checked my blood pressure. "Andrea, what was the last thing you remember?"

Trying to focus my gaze with a pounding headache, I struggled to remember what led to me faint.

"I don't know. I was in Mr. Fitzgerald's class and Ms. Kahn came in and said . . . " My voice trailed off. I remembered. "Daniel is dead." I screamed with tears bursting out of my eyes. Snot was running down into my mouth, and Mama tried to console me, but I was pushing her away. I felt like I was losing my mind.

"Calm down, baby. Mama is here. Shhh. Shhh. Baby. I'm here now."

"Can we take her home?" I heard Auntie Jolie asking the nurse over my cries.

"Well, I would like to ask her a few more questions." "Look at her. Do you think she's in a condition to answer your questions?" There was a calm sternness in Auntie Jolie's voice. "You're right. My apologies. Please take her home."

By the time I reached Mama's car, my shirt was soaked from my tears and sweat. My head felt heavy, and my heart ached. I sat in the backseat in silence but with tears streaming down my face. I could not stop the tears from falling as we drove home. My thoughts were consumed with one question: why did he do it? The image of my friend's face, contorted with pain and sadness, kept replaying in my mind. I tried to remember our last conversation, the one we had just before he made the decision that changed everything. I thought that I had gotten through to him, that I had convinced him that things would get better.

"Baby, are you hungry?" Mama said as we pulled into our driveway.

I could not speak. I shook my head as I wiped away my tears. A sense of hopelessness and despair had taken over me, robbing me of my appetite and energy. All I wanted to do was curl up in my bed and cry myself to sleep. It was as if my soul had been drained, leaving behind an empty shell. It was hard to explain this feeling to anyone who had not experienced this type of loss. It felt like numbness and emptiness had consumed me.

"Let me know if you need anything, baby. I'm not going back to work until this weekend. I want to make sure you're okay." The worry in Mama's eyes led me to believe that she thought I may commit suicide too, but I had no energy to reassure her that I was not going to.

I walked back to my room, took off my damp clothes, crawled into bed, and wrapped myself up in my covers like a human burrito. As I lay in bed, I could feel the weight of confusion and anger crushing me. All I wanted to do was cry and sleep. And that is what I did.

Time must have escaped me because I woke up to a dark room. The stars from outside my window were the only light that greeted me. I searched around in the darkness for my phone. I could not help but wonder how long I had been lying here. Time seemed to have lost its meaning, and it did not matter anymore. All that mattered was this overwhelming feeling of sadness that had engulfed me.

I avoid turning on the lights or making any noise as I did not want my family to know that I was awake. I wanted to be left alone with my thoughts. I found my phone on my nightstand. Mama must have placed it there because I did not remember having my phone when I left school.

Eleven forty-three was what displayed on my phone. I really did sleep the day away. I had six missed calls, four voice messages, and sixteen text messages. I was too exhausted to even check any of the messages.

The thought of never seeing him again and laughing at our inside jokes danced in my head. I closed my eyes and tried to focus on my breathing, hoping it would calm me down. But no matter how hard I tried, the thoughts kept rushing in like a tsunami, one after the other. Tears found their way back to my pillow, and I flipped over the tear-stained pillowcase. And as the night wore on, I hoped I could eventually drift back off to sleep, I knew that tomorrow would be a new day. And I hoped that when I woke up, this heaviness in my chest would have lifted, and I would once again find the strength to face the world. But for now, all I could do was hold on and try to make it through the night.

CHAPTER TWNETY-NINE

PRESENT DAY

I have been able to experience another night of great sleep. I did not think my thoughts will slow down enough for me to have a restful night, but it did. I spent the rest of my Thursday going back and forth with myself if I were going to go to Daniel's funeral.

I woke up this morning feeling different. At first, I couldn't put my finger on it. I do my usual of checking my phone and scrolling the Gram for a minute and then lay in bed. But this morning, I did not wake up with the thoughts of dread and negativity. When I scroll through the Gram, I do not judge people or hate them because they look happy. I feel a little lighter. The weight of grief and sorrow that has been constantly weighing me down seems to have lifted ever so slightly. I cannot believe it. Was this what people meant when they say time heals all wounds? It certainly does not feel like the pain is completely gone, but it is definitely more bearable. And for the first time since Daniel's death, I feel a glimmer of hope.

Of course, I still think about Daniel constantly and miss him terribly. And my besties and I are not in the best place. But there is a subtle shift in my heart. I realize that even though Daniel is no longer physically with me, he will always be a part of me. And instead of dwelling on his absence, I should cherish the memories we shared and carry him with me in my heart. I think about how one small moment can have such a profound impact.

This new feeling has made me feel a little bit hopeful, and for the first time in a while, I want to get out for a walk. I have the feeling like I am coming out from under a powerful spell, and I need to get some fresh air.

Heading to my closet, I know I want to wear a comfortable and easy outfit for the day. So I decide to go for a low-maintenance look. I finger comb my hair into a low bun; it is effortless yet chic. Plus, with the warm weather outside, the bun will help keep me cool. Then I grab my favorite pair of black leggings. They are my go-to for any casual day. Not only are they comfortable, but they also go with almost anything. I pair them with an oversized long- sleeve T-shirt Auntie Jolie brought from New Orleans. The shirt is loose and flowy, providing the perfect balance to the snug fit of the leggings. It is also a light material, perfect for the warm weather today. As I get dressed, I admire my outfit. It is simple yet put together.

After sliding my cell phone into the side pocket of my leggings, I grab my shades and prepare to accomplish a task I did not think I could do for a while. Walking toward the kitchen, smells of Southern cuisines tickle my nose. Scents of candy yams, greens and fried foods envelop the front half of the house.

With tunes of Mary J. Blige thumping through the Bluetooth speaker, I try to get mama's attention. "Ma. Ma." By the third time, I yelled, "Ma!"

"Yeah, what is it, Drea?" she says, balancing the flour while turning down the music.

"What are you in here doing?"

"What does it look like? I'm cooking." "On a Friday?"

"Oh, you mind your business," she says, chuckling. "How are you feeling, honey bunny?"

"Better. I'm about to go for a walk around the neighborhood."

"Oh, you are? I'm glad you're getting out this house." "Yeah. I just need some fresh air."

"Are you sure you're okay?"

"Yes, ma'am. I'm positive."

"Did you finish all of your schoolwork?" "Yes, ma'am. Where is Auntie?"

"Oh, she went to go run a few errands, she'll be back soon.

And you hurry back too. I have a surprise for you." "A surprise? For me?"

"Yes, now go on for your walk so you can come back."

"Alright. I'm just going to walk around the block or so in the opposite direction of the school. I really don't feel like seeing anybody I know."

"I understand. I'll be here when you get back." "You don't have to work tonight?"

"Nope. I don't go back until Monday night."

Did I enter a parallel universe? I feel well enough to go for a walk while Mama is at home listening to music and cooking. This almost feels like how it used to be before the divorce.

"Okay. See you later."

Stepping outside in the warm air felt energizing. The sun kisses my forehead as I make my way down the sidewalk. I stroll aimlessly, not looking at my phone, but taking in the sights of nature around me until I end up at the neighborhood park. I observe the beauty all around me: the bright green trees, the flowers in full bloom, and the birds singing their sweet melodies. It is a reminder that life is full of ups and downs, but there is always something good to hold onto. With each step, the resentment toward Daniel taking his life slowly starts to fade away.

Walking always seemed to have a therapeutic effect on me, and this time is no different. The sound of my own footsteps echo in my ears, and my mind becomes clearer and calmer. I have been holding onto this grudge for far too long, and it was eating away at me from the inside. It was like carrying a heavy burden on my shoulders, weighing me down and preventing me from moving forward. This weight also nudged itself between my important friendships, threatening to destroy those too. But as I continue to walk, I realize that I do not want to carry that burden any longer. I am tired of feeling bitter and angry all the time. I want to let go and find peace within myself. With each step, I start to reflect more on Dr. E and Auntie Jolie's words. Through all the tears and sadness, I find a new sense of understanding and compassion toward others who are hurting like me, specifically Daniel.

I make my way to the empty swing and sit down lightly before pushing myself with my feet. As the swing gets higher, I can feel the cool breeze against my face. Then I feel a smile creep up, and it nearly scares me. I let the swing slow down, and my thoughts slow down. Did I just smile again? Maybe Dr. E was completely right. I am getting stronger. In this very moment, I hear my breath, and as I exhale, I release it all.

"I forgive you Daniel, and I really miss you."

Familiar tears start to form in my eyes, but the feeling associated with the tears are of letting go. I feel a sense of relief. It is a strange feeling, but it is as if the tears are helping me release all the hurt and disappointments that have been consuming me for so long.

I close my eyes and take a deep breath, trying to gather my thoughts. It has been a rough couple of weeks for me, filled with hurt, disappointments, and countless what-ifs. But at that moment, with the sun shining down on me and the gentle breeze whispering through the trees, I finally feel like I am letting go of all the negative emotions. I open my eyes and notice a beautiful black, blue, and yellow butterfly fluttering around me. It seems to be dancing in the air. I smile as it lands on my knee, almost as if it is trying to comfort me. Something in my inner being tells me it is Daniel, and I feel comfort in knowing he is okay.

Sucking in the air around me as I grip the chains on the swing a little bit tighter, I feel the tightness in my chest relax. I have become too familiar with the pressure thumping at my heart since the day I found out about Daniel's suicide, and now I am finally getting some relief. Now I know that butterfly was Daniel. Checking my phone, I start to head back home. I did tell Mama I would not be gone too long. Besides, I do not want to ever pass up the opportunity to eat some of Mama's home cooking.

The cool breeze gently brushes against my skin, bringing more calmness and peace to my emotions. It is funny how a simple walk can clear my mind and put things into perspective. All week, I had been going back and forth over multiple decisions, unsure of what to write in my letter to Daniel and if I were going to attend his funeral and memorial. But as I take in the beauty around me and remembered that butterfly, I realize that I finally have a clear mind to make a decision. I was grateful for this moment of solitude. It is just me and my thoughts, and I am ready to face them head-on.

Turning the corner to my block, I can see in the distance my auntie has made it back because her car is parked behind Mama's car. Climbing the stairs to my porch, I can hear a familiar voice coming from inside the house. Auntie Jolie left the wooden door open, allowing the savory smells of Mama's cooking to escape through the screen door. Coming closer to the door, I can still hear a voice coming from the living room, but it is muffled and distant. It is a familiar voice, one that I have heard countless times. But it cannot be the person I was wishing for.

"Hey, baby girl," the voice said as I walk in the house, nearly stumbling over my own feet because I cannot believe it.

"Daddy!" I yell, leaping into his arms like I was five years old all over again. I hug his neck so tightly as he pats my back, indicating he cannot breath. "Daddy, what are you doing here?" I ask, still in his arms with tears forming in my eyes.

"I came to see you." He let my feet find the floor before he releases me. "Jolie picked me up from the airport."

I look over at Auntie Jolie and Mama, who were both standing in the door to the kitchen. Auntie Jolie has her arms folded like she is satisfied with maintaining the secret of a lifetime. Mama holds a dish towel with a look I do not see her have often. She does not look tired. She looks happy, like the night of the spring dance.

"You two did this?" I ask, walking over to them and giving them a group hug.

"Guilty," Auntie Jolie says with a sly laugh.

Daddy's easygoing disposition comes back like nothing ever happened. "Get over here and let me take a look at you. Let's see. I haven't seen you in a long time. How long has it been? Five or six months?

I giggle at his exaggerated calculations. "Daddy, I saw you for Christmas."

"That was a long time ago," he says, hugging me again. "Alright, you two. I worked too hard making this food. Plus, I'm starving."

Daddy and I look at each other. "The drill sergeant has spoken," he says with a sly smile.

We all sit down at the kitchen table as Mama prepares to serve us. Familiar feelings start to bubble up inside of me. It has been a while since we were all under one roof and eating at the kitchen table together.

"Where is Franklin?"

"Franky has to work Saturdays and Sundays. He couldn't get the days off."

"You've always been harder on Franklin than Drea," Mama says, placing Daddy's plate down in front of him.

"You know just as well as I do that Franky needs more guidance than Drea. And he needs it from a man."

"Yeah, I guess. I just miss my baby."

"Your baby will be down here this summer."

"He will?" I ask, trying to juggle biscuits and gravy in my mouth while I talk.

"Yeah, just for a couple of weeks. Bianca, this food is delicious."

"Thanks, Shane."

Mama and Daddy exchange a caring look between each other.

"Daddy, how long will you be here?"

"Just over the weekend. We have testing coming up next week, and I must be there. But not before I see my baby girl." We both smile. My dad and I will always have a special bond. Mama once told me that Daddy knew the exact day I was going to be born. And when I finally came on the day he predicted, I would only stop crying when Daddy held me. Me and daddy are like these biscuits and gravy, we just belong together.

"Your mama told me what happened to your friend Daniel. How are you feeling?"

I can see and feel everyone's eyes shift to me. "I'm doing better."

"I know that must have been hard, baby, and I'm sorry you had to go through it. I wish I could have been here earlier."

"Yeah, but I know Daniel is in a better place where he's truly accepted for who he is."

Mama grabs my hand as if I said something profound. "I'm so proud of you."

I look over to Auntie Jolie, who has been quiet since we sat down, and she has a smile of approval on her face.

"I've also decided to go to his funeral tomorrow." "You have?" Daddy asks.

"Yes. After my counseling sessions and talking with Auntie, I've got a new perspective."

Both Mama and Daddy look at Auntie Jolie as she continues to eat, not paying attention to the stares now directed toward her. "Auntie, do you mind coming with me tomorrow?"

"Of course."

We exchange smiles, and she shoots me a wink.

"We can all go and show our respects," Mama chimes in. "No. mama, I prefer you and Daddy stay behind. It's already going to be packed with so many students coming just to be nosey."

Mama and Daddy look at each other, trying to find the reasoning in my decision. And I do not offer any additional comments on my decision. I only hope they can respect it.

Turning to Daddy, I quickly change the subject before Mama can object. "Daddy, I have to finish some homework, but could we watch Akeelah and the Bee?"

"You still love that movie, huh?"

"I love watching it with you and Mama."

Mama looks up from pushing her food around on the plate. "You want me to watch it too?"

"Yes, like we used to do. I miss our movie nights." Mama and Daddy look back at each other. "Auntie, you can join too."

"Why not? Since I'm already here to support you, Drea, let's do it," Daddy says.

"Thanks, Daddy. Mama, the food is delicious. May I be excused?"

"Yes, go ahead." She has a look of confusion and uneasiness.

I am not sure if it is because I do not want her to come with me to the funeral or because I want to have a family movie night. But I left the table feeling satisfied and ready to complete Dr. E's homework assignment.

CHAPTER THIRTY

I remember when daddy used to play a lot of Michael Jackson music when I was in elementary school. But the one song that always stood out to me was "Man in the Mirror." It stuck with me because I remembered the video and Mama and Daddy would talk about how inspiring the words were. It was not until I got older that those words resonated with me. As I look into the mirror, I see a person who is both familiar and unfamiliar to me. It is like I know this person who is staring back at me, but at the same time, there is something different about her. It is like she has grown and changed in some way that I cannot quite put my finger on. And as I continue to get to know her, I realize that she is much stronger and more in control of her emotions than before.

It is funny how we think we know ourselves so well, yet every day we are evolving and changing in ways we cannot always see or understand. And it is in these moments of self-reflection, when we look at ourselves in the mirror, that we truly begin to understand the person we are becoming.

The girl I see in the mirror today has been through a lot. She has faced challenges, experienced heartbreak, and endured tough times. But she has also overcome them all, one day at a time. She emerged from the darkness with a newfound strength and resilience that she did not know she had. The person staring back at me now is still afraid to take risks but is at least willing to try. She has learned to embrace her mistakes and turn them into opportunities for growth. She does not let fear hold her back, and instead, she faces it head-on. It is like she has unlocked another level of confidence that was dormant within her. And like the song "Man in the Mirror" and Dr. E and Auntie's advice, I am going to make a change by starting with myself.

I used to be ruled by my emotions, often getting overwhelmed and unable to handle them. But now, I am learning to step back and calmly assess the situation. I try not to allow my emotions to consume me, but instead, I take control of them and use them to my advantage like through writing. This person in the mirror has taken the time to get to know her thoughts, feelings, and desires. She has learned to be honest with herself and has worked hard to become the best version of herself. Of course, she is not perfect. She still has her flaws and struggles, but she does not let them define her.

"You look nice, honey," Auntie says, standing in my door. I jump because I was so consumed by my thoughts of self-discovery, I lost all concept of time.

"Thanks. Is it time to go?" "Yep. I'm ready when you are."

I turn back to the mirror to give myself one final approval. It is not the black and white peplum dress I am wearing or my neatly structured low bun that gives me the approval I am looking for. I approve of my strength.

With a deep exhalation, I turn back to Auntie. "I'm ready." Mama is sitting in her favorite La-Z-Boy recliner chair while Daddy sits on the sofa next to his pillow and blanket he used last night. Once he saw me come into the living room, he jumps up so quickly, his pillow tumbles down to the floor.

"Are you okay, Drea?" "Yes, I'm good, Daddy."

"Are you sure you don't want your mother and I to go with you?"

I look at Mama and Auntie and back at Daddy. "I'm sure. I want you two to stay here."

I secretly would not mind if they had some alone time together and maybe have their own self-discovery. I mean, if a fifteen-year-old can do it, I would think an adult would be able to do it without any problems.

"Come on, Drea. We don't want to be late," Auntie says, directing me to the door.

"I'll see y'all when we get back."

"We will be right here, baby," Mama says, getting up to hug me. "I love you."

"Love you too."

Pulling up to the church is more of a who's who event than a funeral. I roll my eyes at the sight before me. Kids from my school are there, along with teachers and even some community leaders. It is like a scene out of a circus. To be honest, I do not personally know most of the people who are outside. Some of the students here I recognize from my school, but I never really talked to them. And as for the adults, they are faces I had seen in passing, but I never really paid much attention to them. I am annoyed by the whole situation. It is clear that most of these people are here to be nosey and to be seen. I mean, why else would they come to a person's funeral they did not know or help belittle when he was alive?

I let out a sigh as I step out of Auntie's car. "Drea, you good?"

"Yes, ma'am. I was expecting this."

"You mean all the nosey-ass folks who are only here to spectate and stir up gossip even more? These folks ain't got nothing better else to do. But you know why you're here, and that's what's important."

"Yeah, you're right. I never thought people would use a funeral to still keep up mess."

"It's unfortunate, but some people just don't have anything else going on with their life except to keep up mess."

As we make our way toward the entrance of the church, I can feel myself getting overwhelmed by the crowd and the noise. People are chatting while small kids run around and play. It is chaos. We try to navigate our way through the sea of people.

"Excuse me. Excuse me. May I get by? Excuse me." When we finally make it inside the church, we go to view Daniel's body. I do not think I have ever seen a dead body before, and it sucks the first one must be one of my best friends. I miss him so much, and for a moment, my body is paralyzed as I stand looking at him. I cannot believe it, but he is really gone.

Auntie gently grabs me by the shoulder and directs me to a seat in the middle of the church. She tries to distance ourselves from the crowd. The scene inside the church is the opposite from the circus we went through to get inside. The air is heavy with grief. I look over and notice who must have been relatives of Daniel. He never talked much about his family except how much he could not wait to get away from them.

I look over at the other side of the church and see Noelle and Harmony. We acknowledge each other with a smile. It means the world to me that they would come to his funeral, even though we are not on the best of terms. As I continue to sit, trying to distract myself, all of our conversations start to rush back to me. This is the same church he had to come to every Saturday in hopes of "praying" his gayness out. But it is also the place where he met Christoper. He was so happy then.

The more I think about Daniel, tears start to stream down my cheeks. It has not been a full two weeks since Daniel passed away.

And here we are, gathered to say our final goodbyes.

Auntie Jolie hands me a tissue as she notices me crying. "You okay?"

"Yeah. I'm going to get through it."

"Let out whatever you need to. I got you."

Her words are reassuring, and I know she did have me. "Thank you, Auntie."

As the choir begin to file into the choir stand, Daniel 's parents and his grandparents walk in. Mrs. Gardner looks so elegantly fragile with her hair perfectly arranged hair into a low bun. She wears a beautiful dark blue dress that shows her fragile frame.

But Mr. Gardner really catches my attention. His eyes are empty, as if his soul has been snatched out and someone else is controlling his limbs. Tears begin to fall again from my eyes. I cannot imagine what Daniel's parents must be feeling and thinking throughout this.

"Let me know if you need to get up for some fresh air." Auntie leans over to whisper.

I nod as I wiped my already wet face.

The service begins, and my heart starts to race. I knew that it would be a difficult day, filled with memories and emotions. But I am determined to make it through without breaking down. It is something that I need to do for myself and for Daniel. The pastor speaks, sharing stories and memories of Daniel's life. I smile through my tears as he talks about how meticulous and well-dressed he used to be. I can almost hear Daniel's agreement echoing in the church, and it brings me comfort. Family members stand up to share their own memories of Daniel, and I find myself laughing and crying along with them. They speak of his kindness, his humor, and his unwavering love for other people. It is clear that Daniel had touched the lives of many people, but I am not sure if he ever knew or felt that. I wish he did. Maybe he would still be here today.

But as the service goes on, I feel a sense of pride growing within me. I am proud that I had made it this far without breaking down. I am proud that I am able to hold myself together in front of his family who loved Daniel just as much as I did. But most of all, I have peace knowing that he is okay. The butterfly I saw yesterday confirmed it. I reflect on all the times we had supported each other through difficult moments in our lives. We had always been there for each other, no matter what. And even though Daniel is no longer physically with me, I can still feel his support and love surrounding me.

It is the peace I need to get me through his funeral. And seeing Harmony and Noelle at Daniel's funeral reassures me that I do have a support group who truly loves me.

"Why didn't you speak to Daniel's parents before leaving?" Auntie Jolie asks as we walk to the car. "You didn't want to show your respects to them?"

"I didn't feel like speaking to them."

"Now, Drea, don't you think that's kinda of rude? I mean, they are his parents, and you've been in their home."

"I know," I say before taking a long pause to gather my thoughts. "I don't want to be mean, but I'm not ready to face them yet. Especially because I know how they felt about Daniel's sexuality. I lowkey blame them for his suicide. They never supported him."

"Well, whatever their reasoning was, they still lost a child." "Yeah." I bite my bottom lip before picking at the dry skin that I keep lifting up. "I'm not saying I won't ever speak to them, but today wasn't it."

"I have to respect your decision whether I like it or not. But how are you feeling overall? I mean, from the funeral."

"Good, I guess. I was really glad to see Harmony and Noelle."

"Did you know they were coming?"

"No. We really haven't talked that much this week or last week. But despite our differences, they still showed up for me."

"That's what true friendship is about. I'm so glad you've found a set of friends who are loyal. Speaking of, have you spoken to, ugh, what's his name? The guy who walked you home?"

"Who? Oliver?"

"Yes. Oliver. Have you spoken to him? I didn't see him at the funeral."

It was not until that moment that I allowed my thoughts to rest on Oliver. I realize that I have not given much thought to my boyfriend. It is not that I do not care about him. My mind has been so consumed with understanding and processing my own feelings that I have not had the time or energy to focus on him since the news of Daniel. It is funny how easily we can get lost in our own thoughts and emotions, often neglecting the people around us. I have been so wrapped up in trying to make sense of everything going on inside of me that I have not taken the time to check in with Oliver and see how he is doing.

"No, I haven't. Man, I feel kinda bad too."

"Well, I'm sure he can understand you've been going through some things right now, and he's probably giving you some space."

"I don't know. I don't know the dos and don'ts in a relationship."

"Relationship? Wait. Is Oliver your boyfriend?"

I instantly feel a slight tinge of embarrassment. Yes, I have a boyfriend, and while my close friends may know about him, the idea of someone outside of that inner circle knowing still makes me blush. I do not know why it makes me feel this way. Maybe it is because I am a private person when it comes to matters of the heart. Or perhaps it is because I want to keep this special part of my life between myself and Oliver. Whatever the reason may be, the thought of someone else knowing about our relationship makes me feel exposed and vulnerable.

"Yes. I mean, I don't know now, but please don't tell Mama and Daddy."

"Your secret is safe with me, but eventually you'll have to tell your parents."

"I know. I know. And I'll text him later when I get home.

Daddy leaves tomorrow, and I want to spend some time with him." "I totally understand. Just let me know how I can support you."

"Speaking of, when are you going back to New Orleans?" "Wow. You're trying to get rid of me already?"

"No, of course not, Auntie. I was just asking."

"I'm just teasing you. But I'm not sure. I'm came for you.

And when I think my time in this chapter of your life is completed, then I will head back to Nawlins."

"What do you mean chapter?" "This period in your life." "Oh."

Pulling up in our driveway, I cherish my auntie's open conversations. Unfortunately, I have never reached that level of comfortability with Mama. I do not know what it is, but Auntie Jolie can sense things and knows how to talk to me without going from zero to hundred in three point five seconds.

"Thank you, Auntie."

"For what?" she asks, unbuckling her seatbelt.

"For always listening to me. I just wanted to say that." "You are welcome, honey. Are you coming in or staying in the car?"

"No, I'll be in a minute."

"Okay. I let your parentas know you're out here taking a breather or whatever."

"Thanks."

I reach for my phone and do something I said I would do later. I text Oliver.

Hey. Can you talk?

He quickly texts back. I'm at work, but I am always available for you.

I'm so sorry for ghosting you and being such a bad girlfriend.

I understand you're going through a lot. Just know that I love you.

His words send a wave through my entire body, one that I enjoy.

I love you too.

Chapter Thirty-One

Today, May 2023

Seventh period bell rings. I did it! I really did it! Today was a big day for me. For the first time, since my panic attack, I managed to make it through a full day at school without falling apart. No tears, no hyperventilating, no crippling anxiety. And let me tell you, it feels pretty damn good. Do not get me wrong; it was not easy. Everywhere I turned, there were reminders of him: Daniel's empty desk in our classes and the spot we always used to sit during lunch, now occupied by people I barely know. It was tough, but I am slowly learning how to deal with these triggers. It has been a couple of weeks since we found out Daniel committed suicide. A couple of weeks of sleepless nights, endless tears, and an overwhelming feeling of loneliness. I miss him every single day, but I know he would not want me to wallow in sadness forever. He was always the one pushing me to be stronger and to face my fears. So today, I make the conscious decision to put on a brave face and face my fears.

And now, as the day comes to an end, I am preparing to attend Daniel's memorial service. It is going to be tough but necessary. I need to say my final goodbyes and find closure.

Principal Braun cancelled all eighth period classes for his memorial service. As we all are making our way to the gym, I reach into my pants pocket making sure I have the piece of paper that I have worked on since Daniel's passing.

"Yeah, it's there," I whisper to myself.

"Drea, wait up," Harmony says, maneuvering her way through the crowd of students. "How are you doing?"

Without saying a word, I hug her. Our embrace is genuine. "I'm good. Better."

Harmony looks at me and says, "Look, I know we have been through a lot over the past couple of years, but you're my sister and I don't want anything to ever come between our friendship."

"You're right, and I'm sorry for not always being around."

"Girl, that don't matter. We're here, and you're one of my best friends, Drea."

"Same."

"So we good?" Harmony says, extending out her arm.

"Super good," I say, interlocking my arms with hers.

As we stroll down the hallway, passing by the sounds of students chatting and lockers slamming, I feel reconnected to her. I missed her and Noelle. I did not know how much I needed them until I needed them.

"Where is Noelle?" I say, turning to Harmony. "Oh, she's already in the gym, saving our seats."

Entering the gym, I see Noelle looking effortlessly cool with her loose curls pulled up into a messy bun. She is sitting on the third bleacher from the top, casually scrolling through her phone. As soon as she sees us, she flashes a bright smile at us and waves. As we reach the bleachers, Noelle taps the seat next to her, gesturing for us to sit down.

"Thanks for saving our seats," Harmony says, climbing over the bleachers.

"You know I had to get in here earlier to claim our seats."

"Yeah, thanks," I say, giving her a hug. Noelle looks so surprised and taken aback. Neither of one of us are the most physically affectionate people, but I felt like I just needed to hug her.

"What was that for?"

"It's been a wild year, and I haven't always been the best friend, and I'm sorry."

She gives me a cold stare, and it feels like she is piercing my soul with her eyes. But then, unexpectedly, she pulls me into a hug. Without saying a single word, Noelle accepted my apology. She did not need any explanations or promises that it would not happen again. She simply forgave me with a hug. That hug means the world to me, and I know our friendship was back on track.

This entire school year has taught me some valuable lessons about friendship and forgiveness. My friends could have easily held a grudge and let our friendship dissolve because of my mistakes. But they chose to forgive and move on. That is what true friends do. I love my girls. And although we may argue and stop talking for some time, they are my sisters and we will always ride together.

"Alright, students, take your seats. Everyone find a seat. We are about to get starte,." Principal Braun says, dressed in a checkered brown pants suit that givve her an air of authority, almost like a cop. The students, including myself, can not help but wonder if she were going to start barking orders and criticizing our behavior. But as she stands before the student body and begins her speech, it is clear that her tone of voice is empathetic. It sets the students at ease and makes us feel like we are listening to a friend rather than our principal.

She clears her throat. "First of all, I want to say thank you to everyone for being patient and resilient as we navigate this difficult time of losing a student. I know that some of you were also able to make it to his funeral last Saturday, and I want to take a moment to honor Daniel once again. It's never easy saying goodbye to someone so young and full of life. We may never understand why things like this happen, but we can take comfort in knowing that Daniel will always hold a special place in our hearts." She pauses while adjusting the cord of the microphone.

"Suicide is an incredibly difficult topic to discuss. The thought of someone feeling so overwhelmed and hopeless that they see no alternative but to take their own life is heartbreaking. It's a tragedy that continues to occur far too often, and it seems that no one is immune to its grasp. That's why here, at Oak Valley Hight, we have made it our mission to not only support those who are struggling with the thoughts of suicide, but also to prevent another precious life from being lost. But despite these incredibly difficult emotions, we must push forward and try to make a positive impact in the wake of such a tragedy. That's why we have counselors on staff for you all. We understand that sometimes talking about our struggles can help alleviate some of the weight we carry. Our counselors are here to listen, provide support and guidance, and help individuals work through their emotions and thoughts. We want everyone to know that they are not alone and that there is always someone there to talk to. Furthermore, we want to take a proactive approach in preventing another precious life from being lost to suicide. We know that there is no easy solution when it comes to suicide prevention. It's a complex issue that requires a combination of support, resources, and understanding. But we believe that by working together and supporting one another, we can make a difference."

Applause from everyone cuts through the tense air. But no one wants to look at each other either. We all know some of us may have tears forming in our eyes or already rolling down our faces.

Principal Braun continues, "Now, I want to offer the floor to anyone who would like say anything. Any words of encouragement."

I can sense that no one seems to have the courage to break the silence. And as I look around, I realize that it is up to me to take the first step. I am nervous and not entirely sure if I will read everything from my letter, but I refuse to let this opportunity slip away. Because the truth is, our voices matter. My voice matters. So, with my heart racing and my palms sweating, I gather my courage and stand up. All eyes turn toward me, and for a brief moment, I feel a surge of panic. But then I remember that we are all in this together. I take a deep breath and prepare to share the homework Dr. E assigned me on my first counseling session. The one assignment that had me struggling in my own emotional conflict. And now not only did I complete the assignment, but I am about to read it to the entire student body.

My hands continue to shake as I walk toward the middle of the gym next to Principal Braun.

"Are you okay to do this?" Principal Braun asks me. I nod in reassurance. She hands me the microphone. "Here you go."

With my eyes closed, I take in a deep breath and let it out slowly. "Hello." My voice sounds raspy to me, but I continue. "Hello! My name is Andrea Ramsey, and I am a sophomore here at Oak Valley. Daniel Gardener was one of my best friends. In a society where conformity is often prized, people like Daniel are rare gems. They bring fresh perspectives and ideas that challenge traditions and pave the way for innovation. Daniel's out-of-the-box thinking and complex nature may have made some people uncomfortable, but he was trying to be true to himself." I briefly pause before continuing. "Society wasn't ready to receive his authentic self, and I guess he got tired of trying to fit into a world that didn't support him. I remember the day I found out about his suicide. It felt like the world came crashing down on me, and I was left with nothing but anger and pain. I couldn't believe that the person I loved and cherished was gone. But as time went by, I realized that my anger and frustration toward Daniel were spilling over to other areas of my life. I found myself lashing out at others for no reason and withdrawing from those who cared about me." I look up toward Harmony and Noelle as they shoot me smiles of confidence. "It took me some time to realize that all of this anger was actually directed toward Daniel, and I was taking it out on everyone else. So, Daniel, since you're not here, I hope you can hear my voice. As I reflect on my actions, I understand that holding onto this anger is not doing me any good. It's only causing more pain and hurt. Forgiveness doesn't mean forgetting what happened. It also doesn't mean that what he did was okay. It simply means letting go of the anger and choosing to move on. So, here I am, forgiving you for leaving me. It's not going to be easy, but I understand you didn't feel accepted.

"Acceptance from people is needed especially when you're doing something different from crowd. And we may not always understand what or why a person may do something, but at least be there to listen without judgement."

I continue, "I don't know what my future may hold, but I know Daniel changed my life, and he will forever be in my heart. And so, I'm making a choice to let go of the past and move forward. Granted, it isn't easy, but it is necessary for my own well-being. I'm making a conscious effort to focus on the present and not dwell on the hurt. It isn't easy, but it is a step toward healing and finding myself again. And now I realize that, sometimes, the most difficult lessons are also the most important ones."

A standing ovation from the entire student body warms my heart. And as I scan the crowd, I could have sworn I see Daniel clapping too.

THE END

www.ingramcontent.com/pod-product-compliance
Lightning Source LLC
Chambersburg PA
CBHW030246130626
46549CB00002B/408